YOUR NEXT CAREER

Second Edition

Do What You've Always Wanted to Do

Gail Geary, J.D., CMC

Your Next Career, Second Edition

© 2010 by Gail Geary

Published by JIST Works, an imprint of JIST Publishing
7321 Shadeland Station, Suite 200
Indianapolis, IN 46256
Phone: 800-648-JIST   Fax: 877-454-7839   E-mail: info@jist.com

Visit our Web site at www.jist.com for information on JIST, free job search tips, tables of contents, sample pages, and ordering instructions for our many products!

Quantity discounts are available for JIST books. Please call our Sales Department at 800-648-5478 for a free catalog and more information.

Trade Product Manager: Lori Cates Hand
Interior Designer: Amy Peppler Adams
Page Layout: Toi Davis
Cover Designer: Honeymoon Image + Design
Proofreader and Indexer: Jeanne Clark

Printed in the United States of America
14 13 12 11 10 09   9 8 7 6 5 4 3 2 1

Library of Congress Cataloging-in-Publication Data
Geary, Gail, 1943-
  Your next career : do what you've always wanted to do / Gail Geary. --
2nd ed.
        p. cm.
  "Previous edition published under the title: Over-40 Job Search
Guide."
  Includes index.
  ISBN 978-1-59357-671-4 (alk. paper)
  1. Job hunting. 2. Middle-aged persons--Employment. I. Title.
  HF5382.7.G43 2010
  650.14084'4--dc22
                                    2009016584

We have been careful to provide accurate information in this book, but it is possible that errors and omissions have been introduced. Please consider this in making any career plans or other important decisions. Trust your own judgment above all else and in all things.

Trademarks: All brand names and product names used in this book are trade names, service marks, trademarks, or registered trademarks of their respective owners.

ISBN 978-1-59357-671-4

CONTENTS

CONTENTS

CONTENTS

CONTENTS

CONTENTS

About This Book

As a mature adult seeking a new career or starting an entrepreneurial venture, you have two choices: You can unconsciously sabotage yourself through fear, overconfidence, pride, and so on. *Or* you can be your own best friend in your career search and "wow" a future employer with your impressive, updated resume; your stylish and energetic self-presentation; and your savvy interview skills. Fortunately, you don't have to do it on your own. You have Gail Geary to help you.

In this book, Gail gives you the insider's slant on what works and what doesn't. Her knowledge comes from over a decade of presenting workshops and coaching clients in the midst of career transitions. She has worked with major corporations and their clients as well as individual clients in every industry sector, including finance, transportation, manufacturing, automotive, retail, and healthcare.

With Gail's expert advice, you can establish a new career, revise your vision, or totally reinvent yourself.

Your Next Career is the premier career-transition guide for those seeking a second or next career, devoted exclusively to providing effective solutions for your career-transition needs. It is filled with case studies, clear examples, and interactive exercises, which provide truthful answers to your career-development issues. Welcome to an exciting and enriching read.

INTRODUCTION

You hold in your hands the most comprehensive guide to fulfilling second careers. *Your Next Career* provides concrete how-to information for job seekers as well as budding entrepreneurs. How do you know that you can rely on this guide to meet your needs?

This book is the work of one of the most respected experts in career transition. The previous edition of this book (titled *Over-40 Job Search Guide*) has become the preferred reference guide for mature job seekers and entrepreneurs. So why a second edition? Dramatic changes in the employment market fueled by economic downturn and global competition have fueled the need for a refocus on second careers, but with increasing emphasis on contractual employment and entrepreneurial ventures. The new edition will also meet the needs of those under 40 who are transitioning into second careers.

About the Author

For the last decade, author Gail Geary has consciously chosen an entrepreneurial practice composed of business and career consulting. She regularly conducts continuing-education seminars and has been on the adjunct faculty for the American Management Association and three Atlanta-area universities. On a daily basis, Gail presents career-transition workshops and coaches individual career-transition clients through career and entrepreneurial assessments, resume and CV development, self marketing, and interview and negotiation practice. For the last seven years, she has conducted a special workshop, "How to Use Age as an Advantage in Your Career Search." As if that weren't enough, Gail is a member of the Georgia and Atlanta Bar Associations and uses her expertise to keep abreast of legal issues regarding careers, particularly those involving age and gender discrimination.

Gail knows firsthand what she's teaching others. She successfully transitioned from a career as an English, speech, and drama teacher to the position of corporate counsel for the Aon Group (Alexander & Alexander), an international commercial insurance and human resources consulting firm. She then transitioned into its sales department, becoming the top salesperson internationally out of 17,000 employees and senior vice president of sales and marketing. Her personal experiences in career transition, downsizing, reorganization, and mergers and acquisitions give Gail a practical, as well as academic, perspective.

How Can This Book Help You?

The United States is facing record numbers of unemployed workers due to financial downturns and international competition. There has also been a dramatic downturn in length of employment and permanent employment situations.

During economic downturn, employers achieve immediate improvement in their bottom line when they lay you off, a move that has nothing to do with your performance. Finding yourself out of work, you then face other discouraging hurdles, including discrimination in hiring, a shortage of available jobs for the number of job seekers, entire positions that are rendered obsolete, plus a shortage of permanent employment.

As you transition into your second or next career, you may find your career dreams ambushed by well-meaning family and friends with mistaken impressions about careers that are "age, education, risk, or background inappropriate." And frequently you will also have to address your own negative self-talk. How can you combat these unacknowledged enemies?

In *Your Next Career*, Gail Geary thoroughly prepares you to successfully manage your own career search or entrepreneurial venture development:

- Chapter 1, "Making Future Employment Trends Work for You": This chapter gives you sound information in terms of the future employment market, including the positions and industries that are healthy and hiring now and projected to be so in the future. This chapter also helps you understand how these employment trends are reflected in permanent, shorter-term employment situations and in self-employment opportunities.

- **Chapter 2, "Quantifying Your Passions and Interests":** This chapter provides complete descriptions of formal and informal ways to quantify your passion. It also shares real-life examples of career seekers who discovered and acted on their passions.

- **Chapter 3, "Measuring Your Tolerance for Employment Risk and Entrepreneurial Ventures":** This chapter provides excellent checklists and an entrepreneurial assessment to help you determine whether you have the characteristics of a successful hybrid (nonpermanent) employee or self-employed entrepreneur.

- **Chapter 4, "Designing a Career That Mirrors Your Passions, Interests and Abilities":** This chapter gives you time-tested ways to get started in your next job or entrepreneurial venture. It also teaches you how to avoid the stumbling blocks that can derail your progress toward doing what you've always wanted to do.

- **Chapter 5, "Acquire Inexpensive Skill and Credential Updates":** This chapter shows you how to get the training and certifications you'll need to stay competitive in your current career or move into a new career or a new industry.

- **Chapter 6, "Designing Your *Wow!* Resume":** This chapter shows you how to attract positive attention to your resume while avoiding red flags such as too much experience and gaps in employment. You learn how to design both printed and electronic resumes that will help you land interviews.

- **Chapter 7, "Designing Your *Wow!* Promotional Material":** This chapter expands on resumes to include business cards; standout cover letters; CVs; and additional promotional materials specific to entrepreneurial ventures, including Web sites.

- **Chapter 8, "Strategic Searches Online and Off":** This chapter goes over the various ways of looking for job opportunities and shows you how to maximize your time and your results.

- **Chapter 9, "Achieve Memorable First Impressions and Ace Interviews":** This chapter shows you how to create a compelling first impression and to avoid the red flags that create a negative first impression. It covers the most difficult interview questions with suggested answers.

- **Chapter 10, "Negotiating Your Best Offer"**: This chapter gives specific steps on how to negotiate your desired salary and benefits. Plus, it includes tips on overcoming your fear of negotiating.

- **Chapter 11, "Too Young to Quit Working: Careers for Post-Retirement Years"**: This chapter presents options for people who are approaching retirement age but don't want to—or can't—quit working.

Take Charge of Your Own Career

Developing your second career (or eighth career) does not have to be painful if you put your career transition in perspective. With your past experience, you have the edge over younger and less experienced workers. It's only a matter of promoting your strengths and watching out for those negative career ambushes. This is an exciting time in which to be living. You have more choices. You can be permanently employed, self-employed, or working in multiple versions of these choices.

Stop listening to the naysayers. Relax; get involved with this book, and get your career on track.

CHAPTER I

Making Future Employment Trends Work for You

When I graduated from Emory University, there were few career choices for women. I could have been a nurse, a school teacher, a librarian, a stewardess, a secretary, or a retail salesperson focused on becoming a buyer. I chose to be an English, speech, and drama teacher because I loved English and was people-oriented. But, as career options for women expanded, I transitioned to different roles, including an insurance claims adjuster, a corporate attorney, a senior vice president of sales, and for the last 16 years, the owner of Atlanta Career Transition.

In contrast to my earlier selection of narrow career choices, today's college graduates are being told by college career counselors that they will have on average 12 different careers in their lifetimes. They will need to continuously update themselves, their skills, and their educational credentials to take advantage of new career trends and their own changing career preferences. This advice applies to all of you who are seeking to transition to a second, third, or next career and do what you've always wanted to do.

With today's accelerated speed of employment change, new career options are created every five years and other career options are rendered obsolete by dramatic shifts in the economy.

In 2005 when I wrote the first edition of this book (titled *Over-40 Job Search Guide*), permanent employment was the most prevalent employment trend. Healthcare, education, and business-to-business services were leading the fastest-growing industry sectors. Major economic shifts at that time included the outsourcing of manufacturing and back-office jobs involving technology. Also, the baby-boomer-and-beyond generations were creating an enormous need for healthcare and related services.

And in one of the smartest and boldest career moves I have seen, Jack, a 59-year-old client who was a former IT executive with an MBA and a six-figure income, entered a two-year program to become a medical technician. His career transition was by no means immediate or painless. The following section is Jack's story.

Jack's Story: IT Executive to Medical Technician

When Jack and I began working together, I recommended that he take a Birkman career assessment, which affirmed his suitability for his past career in technology, as well as his current career in custom cabinetry. The Birkman also recommended positions in other fields, including medical technology. Jack ruminated over his career choices for a number of months, during which time we created an awesome "ageless" IT resume, which he dutifully sent to targeted companies. Later, he shared with me that he felt physically ill when he thought of reentering the corporate job market, so he was not overly diligent.

Behind the scenes, he was investigating the costs and locations of medical technology training and doing custom cabinetry. Money was a stumbling block. His wife wanted to quit work, and they had been dipping into their 401(k) during his two years in custom carpentry. But Jack successfully negotiated with his wife for her to work for two more years while he completed his medical technology training. He did carpentry work on the side and he took a course in anatomy as a prerequisite for beginning school.

This career transition was not "a piece of cake," but rather a rocky road. The process took nine months for him to make a decision plus two years of medical technology training. After career counseling, self-assessment, and negotiation with his family, Jack made a career decision that made the employment trends work for him; he will continue his new career as a medical technician in his 60s, 70s, and 80s, or for as long as he chooses to work.

The Top Employment Trends Through 2016

As Bob Dylan sings, "The times they are a-changin'."

We are a part of a great economic upheaval in the job market, and to understand it and embrace it will cause us to be not only survivors, but to be personally fulfilled and well-heeled survivors.

So what can we unequivocally predict? What can you expect in terms of employment when you are choosing your next career or entering an entrepreneurial venture? Do you have to go to school for two or more years like Jack, or can you reinvent yourself based on your past experience? When are you "too old" for a certain career? One thing is for certain: You can choose from more career options than ever before, and you can choose wisely. But first, take a deep breath and open your mind to what the future holds.

Informed sources indicate that 65 percent of the workforce will be employed, but not as full-time employees. So if you are employed but not as a full-time employee, how will you be employed? Great question.

- **Self-employment:** The U.S. Department of Labor predicts a 14 percent increase in self-employment, which can take the form of a small business or consultancy, a franchise or larger business, or subcontract and adjunct opportunities. In my career-transition business in 2008, I saw a 15 percent increase in clients taking the self-employment route by choice, or by default as accidental entrepreneurs. One of my clients, a major IT recruitment firm, indicates that it has seen a significant increase in requests for contract versus permanent employment.

- **Alternative staffing arrangements:** Companies hire employees for a reduced work week or on an as-needed basis as contractors or adjunct staff. Companies such as Right Management Consultants use this model to keep expenses down and reduce the need for displacing employees when revenue is down. Even with the enormous declines in financial markets in 2008 and 2009, financial institutions are still looking for contract financial executives to fill vacant positions at a rate of $60 an hour.

- **Professional employer organizations:** Companies such as Administaff and Robert Half supply the employer with financial, human resources, and technical staff and services, assuming payroll and healthcare costs.

3

■ **Continued outsourcing, reorganization, and reduction in force:** The United States has the shortest corporate job tenure (an average of two years) of any country in the world, encouraging many workers to look toward entrepreneurial ventures and self-employment to provide greater security than traditional employment.

Also, some industries are rapidly declining while others are surging ahead. In 2008, prior to the meltdown in the financial and housing market, the Bureau of Labor Statistics reported that occupations in rapid decline involved production (manufacturing, foundries), federal enterprises, and fishing. They also indicated that positions surging ahead (by as much as 73 percent) were in professional and related occupations, service occupations, and business and financial occupations. Specific positions targeted to surge ahead included healthcare practitioners; technical positions; and education, training, library, computer, mathematical, science, and healthcare support positions. The largest growth was predicted to involve management, scientific, and technical consulting services.

As this book is going to press, industries and positions surging ahead are in education, healthcare, and with the federal government. Industries and positions in decline involve banking, real estate, construction, and retail, and these declines have affected employment numbers in many other industry sectors. Therefore, it is up to you to stay current with employment trends not only by visiting the Bureau of Labor Statistics Web site (www.bls.gov), but also by reading your local newspaper and keeping up with local and national employment news.

How You Can Find Your Next Career in a Radically New Employment Environment

In 2008, 75 percent of my business came from currently employed individuals; but in 2009, as this book goes to press, 66 percent of my business is from individuals who were recently displaced or unemployed, while 34 percent is from currently employed individuals. My clients want to make a career change for three reasons:

- Security and income stability

- Financial gain and challenge

- Underemployment (related to insufficient responsibility, low salary, and lack of upward mobility)

In many cases, the reasons for making a career change are interrelated. What are your reasons for making a career change?

_____

_____

_____

When you are searching for and developing your next career, take into account these factors: your past education, training, and work experience; your passions and interests for the future; the reasons for your current work dissatisfaction; and the economic employment forecast.

And most importantly, realize that your dream can be played out in permanent employment, part-time employment, or self-employment.

Let's look at profiles of three of my recent clients to see how the preceding factors have influenced their career decisions.

Jo Ann

Jo Ann had worked in retail management for more than 20 years and was shocked to be unexpectedly downsized and denied unemployment by her employer. Fortunately, her honesty and perseverance—with the help of an attorney—paid off. She received unemployment compensation and is now building her new career. These are the factors she considered in selecting a new career:

- **Past education, training, and work experience:** Jo Ann had two years toward a business degree, management training on the job, and steady career progression from retail sales into retail management.

- **Passion and interests:** Her passions and interests included social services and healthcare. Jo Ann had enjoyed an earlier stint working for a physician and had also worked in an assisted-living facility. She thrived on working with the elderly and physically disabled and wanted to make a difference in the lives of others.

- **Career dissatisfaction:** Jo Ann was fed up with retail sales and management because of its lack of financial reward, underemployment, stress from long hours, and performance pressure.

- **Employment forecast.** The employment forecast is excellent for healthcare support services.

After counseling, career assessments, networking, information interviews, and much soul searching, Jo Ann felt that she would go back to school to become a physical therapy assistant with future plans to become a physical therapist while working. However, she realized that in most occupations she would need computer skills, which she lacked. After taking all of the courses associated with Microsoft Office, Jo Ann found and landed a position as an administrative assistant for a construction company that was still thriving. She recently sent me a picture of herself in a hard hat and told me how much she loved what she was doing.

The message here is to be flexible and adaptable. Sometimes an irresistible opportunity comes up that you did not anticipate and you can change your mind and take it.

Robert

Robert has worked his way up to the level of CEO/CFO for a major nonprofit organization. He is making in excess of $150,000 with excellent benefits, annual bonus potential, retirement, and a severance plan in place should he be terminated.

- **Past education, training, and work experience:** Robert has a degree in accounting with post-graduate work in finance. He has a history of increasingly responsible leadership positions in for-profit and nonprofit industries. He has a nice nest egg accumulated from an earlier corporate buyout.

- **Passion and interests:** His passion involves helping children succeed in sports. He played football in college and has done volunteer coaching on the side.

- **Career dissatisfaction:** On the surface, Robert's career looks good, but Robert feels unchallenged, wants greater financial gain, wants to contribute toward something he feels passionate about, and wants more time flexibility.

- **Employment forecast:** Given a climate of continued corporate downsizing, mergers, and acquisitions, self-employment is a strong option for people who are self-directed, have sound management skills, have some savings, and are willing to take a calculated risk.

Robert took the Birkman career assessment to identify his strengths, weaknesses, and career options and also took an entrepreneurial assessment. All assessments affirmed his strengths as a leader and as an entrepreneur suited to buying a franchise or existing business with support in the sales and marketing area. Robert's company is preparing to merge with another company within a year. Robert is buying a recreational sports training franchise with a partner and will participate full time after the merger is complete.

Self-employment is a good choice for the future for those who possess the characteristics of an entrepreneur, which can be measured in an entrepreneurial assessment. Robert will have more control over his destiny as a business owner. With his past management success and with the direction provided by the franchisor, he and his business partner are headed in a winning direction.

Ricardo

Ricardo has had a public relations and marketing business focusing on the environment for the past seven years. He has had many notable marketing and public relations successes, but income has been inconsistent. The unpredictability of his business clashes with his desire to provide his family with a stable income, health insurance, and retirement savings and factors strongly in his desire for a career change. He admits to being distracted in the past by volunteer activities with no financial reward. Now he is ready to either rev up his business success or work for a public relations firm or corporation full time. So how can he do it his way? How does he decide between two options that would be equally agreeable to him if they provided sufficient financial reward and health insurance?

- **Past education, training, and work experience:** Ricardo has a degree in communications and past experience working for a major Chamber of Commerce. His consulting resume indicates major successes in promoting prominent clients' exposure on television and in print.

- **Passions and interests:** Ricardo is passionate about environmental causes. His friends affectionately refer to him as a "tree hugger," and his business and spare time are focused in this direction. He admits to being easily distracted and enjoys a wide range of social activities.

- **Career dissatisfaction:** The issue here is financial security for his family. The question is, can he make his business financially viable or should he be employed full time?

- **Employment forecast:** The employment forecast is strong for employment and self-employment related to "green" organizations and industries.

Roberto completed the Birkman assessment and the entrepreneur assessment. It is clear that his talent lies in marketing and counseling, but he could also be a teacher or a human resources executive. His decision for now is for us to create a resume highlighting his marketing and public relations experience toward a permanent position. This resume will work for both full-time and contract positions. The choice that will win is "the first desirable offer" to put his family in a comfortable position. Of course the resume will be on recycled paper.

Wherever you go, whatever you do, there you are.

Career-Change Stumbling Blocks

These are a few of the many stumbling blocks that can get in your way of a successful career change:

- **Unrealistic expectations:** Many people believe that a new job or a new location will make them happy. One of my new friends had just installed my beautiful new granite kitchen countertop. We were seated at my granite bar drinking cups of latté and talking about the reasons people fail to find a job that satisfies them. He shared with me that his past career had included experiences as a Vidal Sassoon hairdresser and salon owner in London, and a stint as a commercial real-estate agent from Budapest to Melbourne. What he found to be true was that happiness is not about the job or the city you work in, if you are not comfortable in your own skin. "Wherever you go, whatever you do, there you are. I secured happiness in my 40s when I settled down, married, got in touch with my faith, and assumed responsibility for the future. I opened my granite and remodeling business and it has been a great success." After I thanked him for his insight, I asked him if he had time to do my hair and I gave him a copy of my book for his wife.

- **Silo thinking/tunnel vision:** During a recent job interview for contract career consulting, I was asked if I exhibited silo behavior—which meant, was I a team player? Could I have my own business and work successfully with others? I assured them that I enjoyed hunting in packs. As many as a third of my career clients need a second or third career but are resistant to change. They believe that their educational credentials have prepared them for one career and one career only, and dang their age and lack of updated credentials. This pride in position and lack of flexibility is a great stumbling block to their success. I give them a career assessment and show them the numerous career possibilities for the future. They are polite and interested, but stay locked into the past—thus limiting their chance for reemployment.

- **Lack of focus and self-discipline:** Career seekers often describe their future goals and ambitions to me, but sometimes get sidetracked by day-to-day distractions that are either fun or disagreeable, but have no bearing on the future. And so, they are reduced to scrambling for whatever they can find to pay their bills.

What are the stumbling blocks to your future career success? Awareness of what they are and seeking solutions with a career counselor can put your fears to rest.

How Do You Do What You've Always Wanted to Do?

It's clear from the profiles of Jo Ann, Robert, and Ricardo that everyone is special. Each of us has a unique profile that includes our education, training, work experience, passions and interests, and current level of satisfaction or dissatisfaction with our career. We also have individual tolerances for employment risk in terms of considering traditional employment versus nontraditional and entrepreneurial options. We all have minor or major stumbling blocks to our success that must be neutralized. So how do you go about choosing a career option and then doing what you've always wanted to do?

Quantify Your Passions Through a Career Assessment

The first step in this process of choices is to quantify (name and identify) your passions and interests through informal and formal methods, including a solid career assessment. I use the Myers-Briggs (www.mbticomplete.com/en/index.aspx) and the Birkman (www.birkman.com/) assessments. The Birkman is considered the Cadillac of assessments and is more thorough, but more expensive. The Myers-Briggs is solid in terms of career recommendations, is less expensive, but provides less information.

There are many other career assessments of value and there are also significant informal clues for identifying your passions and interests, such as how you spend your money. Look at your credit card and checkbook. Identify how you spend your time by looking at your time commitments. Examining your use of money and time can give you strong indicators for future careers, but can also give you false positives. If I were to base my next career on my recent spending habits and time commitments, I would be a home renovator, an elder-care provider, and a cat sitter; but fortunately, most of my time is spent as a career counselor, a business owner, and an author.

How Do You Spend Your Money?

Take a moment now and answer these questions:

1. How do you spend your discretionary money and your time?

   _____

   _____

   _____

2. What career clues do you find?

   _____

   _____

   _____

The economic employment climate of the future will be made up of more consulting, part-time, and contract positions and self-employment opportunities as businesses anticipate and respond to global competition.

Assess Your Tolerance for Entrepreneurial Risk

The next step after taking a career assessment is to take an employment risk assessment to determine whether you have what it takes to be an entrepreneur. I provide an employment risk assessment for you to take in chapter 3, "Measuring Your Tolerance for Employment Risk and Entrepreneurial Ventures."

Align Your Interests with a Viable Field

The third step is to align your passions and interests with a career or entrepreneurial venture that is economically in demand and available in the career market not only today, but also in the foreseeable future. A combination of formal and informal research is the best way to discover which careers are in demand today and in the future. My sources include books, the Bureau of Labor Statistics, the media, career transition firms, clients, the stock market, recruiters, retained search firms, the Internet, and so on. And I also keep an eye on the most simple research form: the Sunday employment section of the local newspaper. Which positions do you find are in greatest demand? Can you see yourself transitioning into one or more of these fields? Who do you know that works in these fields that you can informally interview?

You might have fallen into your career by accident, because of financial need, or at the direction of parents. Fortunately, second careers can be *conscious* choices, which are more exciting and fulfilling. Read on in chapter 2 to learn how to identify your passions and interests and incorporate them into your new career.

CHAPTER 2

Quantifying Your Passions and Interests

Discovering your passions and interests is the first step in making an informed career choice. This discovery can be done through formal career assessments such as the Myers-Briggs and the Birkman, and also through informal methods such as reviewing how you spend your spare time and your discretionary money.

Informal Exploration

Let's look first at the informal ways of assessing a future career choice. Take a moment to answer the following questions:

1. Are you seeking a second career or next career because you have lost your passion for your current career?

2. Are you seeking a second or next career because you never felt passionate about your first career?

3. Are you seeking a second or next career because the career you were passionately crazy about is no longer available to you in the current job market or does not pay enough money to support your desired lifestyle?

If none of the above describes your situation, write the reason you are seeking a career change in the following box.

```
┌─────────────────────────────────────────────────┐
│              Career Change Reasons                │
├─────────────────────────────────────────────────┤
│  My reason/s for making a career change is/are    │
│                                                   │
│  _____ │
│                                                   │
│  _____ │
│                                                   │
│  _____ │
│                                                   │
│  _____ │
└─────────────────────────────────────────────────┘
```

Free-Time Passions

While reading a recent Atlanta Symphony Orchestra concert program, I noticed that below each musician's picture were listed spare-time passions and interests. These passions ranged widely from skiing, to playing the stock market, to collecting antiques. In many cases these spare-time passions and interests presented a clue to a second or next career option. Susan, an accomplished symphony flutist whose passion was flying, became an international pilot for a major commercial transport airline in her second career. When I interviewed her about her career change, she said that flying was less stressful, more enjoyable, and more lucrative than her career as a musician. Susan is passionate about her career as a pilot, and now her spare-time passions center around playing the flute, supporting the symphony, and skiing. Passions change as we mature, and it is comforting to know that you can identify and express your passions as hobbies and also in new careers.

My spare-time passions are hiking, redecorating my home, and painting pet portraits. My family and friends are in consensus that these passions should remain hobbies. But what do they know? Perhaps their reasons include a broken ankle from hiking and the fact that my folk-art pet portraits look like they were done by my inner child.

What are your free-time passions? Do these suggest a new career option for you as they did for Susan the flutist turned airline pilot? List up to three free-time passions and the career options they suggest.

Free-Time Passions
1. _____
_____
2. _____
_____
3. _____
_____

Where Does Your Money Go?

Another clue to identifying your next career is found in how you spend your discretionary income. This is found in your checkbook or online checking record, and on your credit card statement.

A search of my husband's recent online checking and credit card spending reveals many dollars spent on books, CDs related to nature and war, and sporting equipment such as our kayaks and kayak racks. It should not surprise you that his second, third, and fourth careers have involved being a fitness trainer, teaching outdoor survival classes to children in camps and in after-school programs. He now works for the Small Business Administration assisting disaster victims with home and business loans. This is his all-time favorite career.

It is never too late to realize your dreams, to express your reason for being, to share your passion in a new career.

Now look at your credit card statement and your checking account and identify the top three ways that you spend your discretionary income. List them below as well as the career options they suggest.

Discretionary Spending
1. _____
_____
2. _____

(continued)

(continued)

```
3 _____
  _____
  _____
```

What Work Would You Do for Free?

A third way to identify your passions is to ask yourself this question: "What work/activity would I do if I were not being paid?" Ricardo is the owner of a marketing and communications firm specializing in environmental causes. A self-declared "tree-hugger," Ricardo is so passionate about helping people and promoting environmental causes that he spends his spare time playing in the same arena as his business. He volunteers in multiple positions involving environmental and social causes and consults in communications and marketing for green businesses and organizations.

However, this does not mean that this is the only career choice he has. With the average college graduate predicted to have as many as 12 different careers, Ricardo has a few careers to go. In fact, in his formal Birkman Career Assessment, Ricardo learned that he shares similar interests, needs, and strengths with lawyers, public school counselors, and sales professionals in medical services. When you think about his additional career options, do you see a common thread? I see that Ricardo is interested in influencing, persuading others, and protecting and defending human rights and causes.

Now list three activities that you would do if you were not being paid. What careers do they suggest?

Work I Would Do for Free
1. _____
_____
2. _____
_____
3. _____
_____

Take Small Steps Toward Big Goals

In addition to being a career counselor, I frequently present programs on time management to corporations. One of the pieces of advice I give my clients is to take a small step every day toward realizing your goals and dreams. If you have always wanted to get your engineering degree, order the course catalogue from a nearby college so that you can understand the admission requirements and the time and expenses involved in getting this degree. When you think of reenrolling in a course or college, try to look at it in small increments instead of a painful long haul. Does your company offer tuition reimbursement? Can you take your courses online?

Stumbling Blocks to Career Transition Success

Before I discuss formal career assessments such as the Birkman-Direct and the Myers-Briggs, let's address this question: Why is it that many people continue to work in jobs they find distasteful?

Excuses abound. Psychologists refer to these excuses as fears, new-age writers refer to these excuses as personal demons, and most business-oriented counselors refer to these as stumbling blocks to career success. Let's look together at a few of the most common stumbling blocks to career change that I encounter with my clients.

Fear of Financial Insecurity

In a recent class I taught on how to use age as an advantage in your career search, I pointed out to the class that within the next 10 years most of us will be employed, but not as full-time employees. We may be self-employed or work as adjunct staff, contract workers, part-time workers, and so on. Marie, a former human resources benefit professional, shared that she wanted to start her own HR consulting business; in fact, she had landed several paid contract opportunities in the past. She was financially fearful of starting her consulting business because of the inconsistency of income, the costs to start the business, and the difficulty in obtaining health insurance.

I addressed Marie's three stumbling blocks:

- With corporations reorganizing, merging, and downsizing on the average of every two to three years, there is really no long-term financial corporate security. There is often more financial security in self-employment.

- I pointed out to Marie that the costs to start a consultancy were actually under $1,000, which would include the cost of business cards; a printed one-sheet flyer about the business; and a pre-constructed "write-it-yourself Web site," including hosting costs. I pointed out to her that she could try her own consulting business for six months without breaking the bank and then could rejoin corporate life if her consultancy did not pan out.

- In terms of insurance benefits, many contractors are paying insurance benefits to their subcontractors; group insurance can be found through professional associations, and companies such as Kaiser and Blue Cross/Blue Shield are insuring many self-employed people. I am currently insured for medical benefits under my husband's policy, but I joined the Atlanta Bar Association to purchase reasonably priced disability insurance as part of a group. My brother Rich, a self-employed tennis pro and event organizer, has been insured by Kaiser for a number of years. He has purchased disability insurance from a national tennis association.

Fear of Rejection

Sometimes my clients lose momentum during the career search despite our weekly check-ins. When I ask them who they have contacted and what network meetings they have gone to, they indicate that they have been too busy with the other things in their lives to spend time in the career search. One client's excuses involved a combination of volunteer activities and family events. Another client's excuses involved practicing and playing in a jazz band and computer problems.

The professional volunteer admitted that he hated to be rejected by potential employers. He was praised for his volunteer efforts and this felt better than being rejected. By his admitting this and my understanding this issue, he was able to reenergize himself. We agreed together on a certain number of letters and phone calls per week for him to make to potential employers. He is on track and feeling much more positive about himself and his career transition. As for my jazz-band client, our time is up. I feel like she will be reemployed when her music and her money run out.

Fear of Success

Another reason clients procrastinate is that they know if they put their minds to it, they will succeed in landing almost any job they want—because they have a history of high achievement. But they are asking themselves this question: Is the ultimate payoff worth the effort?

A well-known owner of an Atlanta investment firm contacted me in reference to two of her divorced female clients who needed to be reemployed after a long hiatus of raising children. Their financial support was ending and they had to take care of themselves in the future. One client without a college education took a job at a drugstore in the photography department to train herself in this skill for a more lucrative position in photography later. She was not hung up on her image. The second client was an avid ALTA tennis buff enjoying her position as mom and tennis captain. She appeared to resent the idea of returning to work. The last time we spoke I sensed that she was making rather halfhearted attempts to be reemployed because she knew that she would have to learn computer skills, might have to go back to school, and would at some point have to work full time.

Fear of Failure

Often my older clients, or those with a lack of formal education or a physical disability, will make derogatory remarks about themselves such as, "I think that I'm too old to compete in this arena" or "I wish I had a college education." Recently I was told, "I don't want to apply for that job because I don't feel self-confident because I am missing several of my upper teeth." These are legitimate stumbling blocks.

- In the case of older clients, I help them identify and remove or modify negative stereotypes employers associate with aging, such as grey hair, less than energetic movements, and lack of computer skills. I also help them choose industries and positions that are "age-friendly," such as healthcare and educational environments.

- In the case of clients with a lack of formal education, I often suggest enrolling in short courses through a community college to obtain a certification such as supervisory management training, or a course to become a private investigator.

- In terms of physical disabilities, I have worked with clients who have had strokes, major hearing losses, multiple sclerosis, tooth loss, and obesity. All of these issues have required individual compassionate advice. My stroke victim was a young former Internet guru who, after two years in rehab, was ready to reenter the job market. His physical appearance and voice were somewhat impaired but his brain was excellent. I advised him to explain his situation to his potential employer at the time of the interview, indicating that his brain was as good as ever and that he would be a wonderful employee. For a client who needed dental work, I located a charity dental clinic to remove her remaining teeth and provide her with dentures.

Your Career Transition Fears

What are your own career transition fears? Name those that I have mentioned as well as others I have not. Begin to take action to mitigate and negate them so that you can move on.

1. _____

2. _____

3. _____

4. _____

5. _____

I am an optimistic, self-confident, talented career counselor, and I have yet to work with anyone possessing the physical and mental ability and the desire to work who has been unable to overcome their stumbling blocks to career success. But in all cases, these career seekers availed themselves of support in terms of friends, counselors, books, and career-support networking groups such as Crossroads Career Network (www.crossroadscareer.org) and Re:Focus on Careers (www.refocusoncareers.com).

Everyone who is in career transition experiences fears. I have personally experienced the fears of financial insecurity, rejection, failure, and success, and have been helped along the way by great books, talented counselors, and good friends. Here are some of my favorite book selections that have helped me to overcome my own career-related fears:

- *The Worry Workbook,* by Les Carter, Ph.D., and Frank Minirth, M.D.
- *Spontaneous Optimism,* by Dr. Maryann Troiani and Dr. Michael Mercer
- *The Artist's Way,* by Julia Cameron
- *The Pursuit of Happiness,* by David Myers, Ph.D.

How to Take and Use Formal Career Assessments

Now that you've had a look at informal ways to assess your career goals, and seen some of the stumbling blocks that trip up many career changers, here's a look at the top formal career assessments.

The BirkmanDirect

The BirkmanDirect is considered by many career counselors to be the champagne of career assessments. It has all the bells and whistles to give you a thorough understanding of your behavioral strengths, needs, and interests, and it presents you with multiple career options validated by a database of more than 2 million people who have taken the assessment. You can take this assessment online in about 45 minutes, but you must have a Birkman Certified Consultant interpret your assessment in person or via telephone because the assessment is complex and not self-explanatory. The interpretation takes an average of two hours and provides Internet links for further career research for all career options suggested. The Birkman as well as other career assessments should be taken prior to making a career choice or creating a resume.

The best way to show you what the Birkman reveals and how I use it in career transition is to share how I used this assessment with Dana, a recent client. When I first met Dana, she was an unsatisfied co-owner of a small business. She didn't particularly like the type of business and it was not making enough money to support two people. Her previous career had included nine years in banking with a recent MBA. Her future desire was to combine her experience in banking with her administrative experience managing a small business. She needed help in realizing her dream. I suggested that she take the Birkman assessment so that we could evaluate her career options in light of not only her experience and education, but also in terms of her strengths, needs, and interests.

After Dana took the Birkman online, I printed two copies of it and met with her in person. (In dealing with a distance counselor, this can be handled by telephone, with each party printing their own copy or looking at the results online.) The Birkman is colorful and very thorough—in fact, more than 40 pages. First, we reviewed her strengths, needs, and stress reactions in the following areas, which provided the basis for later career recommendations:

- **One-on-one relationships:** Dana's strength lies in her straightforward approach to others, and she feels less stress when others approach her in the same way.

- **Acceptance:** Dana's strengths include strong communication skills. She is at ease with groups, and is pleasant and outgoing. She prefers a broad circle of friends and acquaintances. Without this support, she may try too hard to please others.

- **Organizing:** Dana is alert to new ideas and combines initiative with procedure. She needs a background of familiarity and support to avoid stress.

- **Authority:** Dana is pleasant, agreeable, self-directed, and low-key in her direction of others. Her needs include a peaceful work environment.

- **Advantage:** Dana is trustful, loyal, and service oriented. She enjoys a certain amount of competition, but face-to-face conflicts cause her stress.

- **Activity:** Dana is enthusiastic, energetic, and forceful but wants to be in control in expending her energies.

- **Challenge:** Dana has a balanced outlook on herself and others, without being either too critical or too self-confident. She is most at ease among others who share her balanced outlook.

- **Empathy:** Dana is objective yet sympathetic and is more comfortable when others treat her in the same way without over-emphasizing feelings.

- **Change:** Dana is responsive to change and can resist interruption, but is less stressed when she is forewarned.

- **Thought:** Dana can make quick and competent decisions and wants the same from others.

- **Freedom:** Dana shows a good balance between independence and conformity. She prefers consistency and predictability.

At this point in my interpretation of the Birkman, we discussed that owning a small business with unpredictable income was not the best fit for her according to her needs. She admitted that she was often in disagreement with her business partner. She wholeheartedly agreed that she would prefer being an employee versus an employer and would like to sell her business as soon as possible.

The Birkman proceeds with a Life Style Grid and then goes directly into the Career Management Report. Below is a very brief description of the Life Style Grid.

Life Style Grid

The second third of the Birkman assessment identifies interests, usual behavior, needs, and stress reactions. In this Life Style Grid we learned that Dana's interests involve innovating, creating, planning, and presenting. When she is working effectively, she is orderly and consistent. Under stress, Dana can become impatient and inflexible.

The Career Management Report: Organizational Focus/Job Families/Job Titles

The first two sections of the Birkman have built upon this final section, which indicates that Dana's organizational focus involves long-term innovative strategy and finance and administration. As we continued into her report, she was very excited to learn what careers the assessment suggested based on her strengths, needs, and interests, which were compared to a database of more than two million people. Here are the careers it suggested:

- Accounting and bookkeeping
- Teaching on all educational levels
- Social service counseling
- Employee relations/training
- Banking and finance
- Administrative activities

Each major category suggests multiple specific position titles with links into the Bureau of Labor Statistics Web site, providing information on salary, future job potential, education, growth, and so on.

Dana's Plan of Action

Dana's plan of action is to sell the business and then have me prepare a resume focused on a position as administrative manager of a small to medium-sized business. After she is gainfully employed, she will take courses in human resource management and will secure HR certifications, including the PHR and SPHR.

The Birkman is not only helpful in making a career decision, but I can use the language describing Dana's strengths in her resume when I write a summary of her qualifications.

Myers-Briggs Type Indicator

The Myers-Briggs Type Indicator is a personality type assessment developed by a mother-and-daughter team in the 1940s and continually updated since that time. More than two million people take the assessment annually and have proven the instrument to be both valid and reliable.

This assessment defines 16 different personality types based on your favorite world (E: extroversion or I: introversion); your focus on basic information or interpretation (S: sensing or I: intuition); your decision-making process (T: thinking or F: feeling); and your preference to get things decided or stay open (J: judging or P: perceiving). There is no preferred personality type, but each of the 16 types has strengths and weaknesses, preferred work environments, and suggested career options.

The Myers-Briggs can be self-interpreted, but a career counselor can help widen the listed choices. For example, clients are often disturbed when they see career choices that they are not interested in—for example, funeral director, veterinarian, or minister. A career counselor can explain that these choices do not have to be taken literally but represent a collection of personality characteristics that are common to other careers. For example, a funeral director might also be good at customer service or sales. A veterinarian might be good as an X-ray technician or a dog trainer. (I know two ministers who have changed careers. One is doing tax preparation as a third career after a second career in sales; another is doing couples and individual counseling as a second career.)

Now let's take a look at one of my clients, Marco, and how his Myers-Briggs results were used in his career search. The Myers-Briggs can be taken online or in person and takes about 30 minutes. The results are less comprehensive than the Birkman, about 14 pages long, but the test is less expensive.

Of the 16 different personality types, Marco tested as INTJ, which is primarily an intuitive introvert with a preference for logic over feeling and structure over flexibility. Marco was a senior programmer with 15 years of experience with an organization that was going through a major reorganization. He hired me to bring guidance and structure to his career search.

The Myers-Briggs confirmed programming as one of his recommended careers, as well as engineering, law, environmental planning, and news editing. Marco was confident that he would not have to change careers but wanted to use the Meyers-Briggs to understand his strengths and weaknesses and best career environment.

Let's take a look at Marco's Objective and Qualifications Summary in his resume. I will boldface some of the words that are his strengths as revealed in the Myers-Briggs.

Objective

Programmer Analyst/Applications Developer/Software Engineer emphasizing **strong analytical skills,** effective oral and written communication, **attention to detail,** and **self-direction.**

Qualifications Summary

Extensive experience in information technology with **specific application experience** in newspaper circulation, call center/telemarketing, database marketing, cellular telephone billing, and payroll/personnel. **Consistently earn job promotions** based on a vast range of programming knowledge and skills.

Even if you are staying in a similar position, the Myers-Briggs assessment confirms your choice and enhances your resume. Plus, it helped Marco understand that he would perform best in a structured environment and that he could be quite comfortable working at his computer screen for hours as well as interacting with his coworkers.

Marco could be a good candidate for virtual office work because of his introversion characteristic.

Knowing that socializing did not come as easily to him as it does to extroverts, Marco developed speaking experience in Toastmasters (www.toastmastersinternational.org) to overcome his fear of public speaking. This background has helped considerably in his job search. He interviews well and is not resistant to networking, which does not come naturally. Although he is in the early stages of his job search, I am confident that all of his preparation will pay off.

Multiple Ways of Discovering Your Passion and Acting on It

By now you know that there are multiple formal and informal ways of discovering what you are passionate about and finding out whether your passion will satisfy your economic needs in today's career marketplace. You can identify your passion through informal ways, such as reviewing your calendar to see how you spend your spare time, and reviewing your checkbook and charge card to discover how you spend your discretionary income. You can also look in your local newspaper or online and circle all of the careers you are interested in investigating. Then you can read more about them in the Bureau of Labor Statistics's *Occupational Outlook Handbook* (www.bls.gov/oco).

In a trendy way to figure out what you like, ask yourself about the content of newsletters you subscribe to, Web sites you visit and blogs you read, books you read, TV programs you select, and movies you view. Do you see evidence that points you to a new career? I enjoy reading and watching murder mysteries, which does not indicate that I will become a private investigator or a mortician in my next career, but does support my previous career as a corporate attorney and my current interest in uncovering my clients' passions and interests.

Formal career assessments are the most objective way to make a career decision, with the Birkman being the most comprehensive and the Myers-Briggs also being very good. Occasionally potential employers will give job candidates a career assessment with the idea that a particular personality type is a better fit for a certain position.

In my former position of senior vice president of sales and marketing, our organization was keen on using a profile called DISC. There were four basic types signaled by the letters, D, I, S, and C. We generally hired *D*s and *I*s for sales positions because of their extroversion, but sometimes a candidate's proven experience outweighed his or her DISC profile and experience won out.

If you want more reassurance that you are making the right choice after you have taken your assessments, you can set up an information interview with an individual working in your position of interest or employing people for the position. One of my clients became a private investigator six months after taking the Myers-Briggs, after having an information interview with a private investigator and taking a six-week course. He is investigating insurance fraud and is a satisfied individual.

Conducting an Effective Information Interview

An information interview can lead to a job interview, but that is not its primary purpose. The primary purpose of an information interview is for you to uncover enough information to decide whether you are interested in pursuing a certain position.

First make an appointment (usually in person) with a hiring manager, a personnel manager, or someone who is currently working in or has recently worked in the position. Make it clear that you are not asking for a job interview. Ask questions interspersed with pleasant conversation so that the person you're interviewing does not feel interrogated. Be very well prepared. Bring your resume if you have one, and business cards if you have prepared these. Give out the resume only if you are satisfied that it will positively assist you in the information interview. You may be best served to prepare it after the information interview.

Cover these questions in your own words:

- What are the educational requirements for this position?
- What are the experience requirements for this position?
- What is the current salary range for this position from entry level to a senior position?
- Is this position currently in demand within your industry? Which companies are hiring?

- What are the hours and conditions for this position?
- What is the future potential for this position?
- Does this position experience frequent turnover or is it being outsourced?

Be very considerate of the person you're interviewing and keep the interview as brief as possible, close to 30 minutes (unless it turns into a job interview at the direction of the interviewer). Before you go to the interview, do research on the position and get a position description. Sources for this include simply typing the position title into Google, typing the title into a job bank consolidator such as Simply Hired (www.simplyhired.com), and going to the *Occupational Outlook Handbook* for a very complete description (www.bls.gov/oco). Generally speaking, a personal information interview will gather more information than Internet research will, but I recommend doing both for maximum information.

And always send a thank-you note after the information interview.

This chapter has provided you with multiple and exciting ways to discover and quantify your passion. You will discover your passion through informal assessments and career assessments. You will quantify it through personal research and information interviews.

When you have discovered and quantified your passion, the next step is to decide how you want to express your passion. For example, I am a self-employed career consultant, an entrepreneurial business owner who takes private clients in career transition and career enhancement in my business, Atlanta Career Transition. For the last seven years, I have also been a part-time employee of Right Management Career Consultants. My passion is played out in these two major arenas as well as my being an author and a corporate presenter. Many of my friends and clients alternate between employment and self-employment. Some of my clients are fully self-employed as business owners. To embrace today's employment trends, it helps to be flexible and adaptable.

Remember that it is never too late to do what you want and that dreams have no expiration date.

CHAPTER 3

Measuring Your Tolerance for Employment Risk and Entrepreneurial Ventures

"In a climate of insecure employment, greater security is often found in self-employment and entrepreneurial ventures."

The following 2009 employment factors clearly support the insecurity of the traditional employment market:

- The average job length has declined to two years.
- Employment in real estate, construction, and financial institutions has dramatically declined.
- Many states have suffered high unemployment rates, such as Michigan (12.6 percent), Oregon (12.1 percent), and South Carolina (11.4 percent).

In light of these employment factors, you will be wise to consider self-employment or an entrepreneurial venture if you have some tolerance for financial risk. In this chapter, you will measure your tolerance for financial risk, learn how to increase your tolerance for risk, and take a look at industries and businesses that have thrived in up and down employment markets. You'll also explore how you can capitalize on the advantages of your age and experience while being alert to the traps that can snare a naive entrepreneur.

Affirming the Advantages of Prior Work Experience

Your age and experience are a distinct advantage to you in an entrepreneurial venture or self-employment. As an experienced worker, you possess a number of specific advantages over someone in the early stages of his or her career. Isn't it about time to have the edge?

Age Advantages in Entrepreneurship

Check the advantages that apply to you:

_____ 1. You have in-depth work or volunteer experience and expertise in one or more areas.

(For example, Mike, a personnel manager for a government agency, has successful experience in interviewing, customer service, and public affairs and has been a volunteer naturalist.)

_____ 2. You have financial reserves that allow you to borrow or raise the necessary money to buy or start a business or franchise and sustain yourself and your family during the startup phase.

(For example, Joan financed a Massage Envy franchise with a small inheritance from the sale of her mother's house. She can sustain herself through personal savings for six months to a year if necessary.)

_____ 3. You have medical insurance in place for yourself and your family or know where to secure it.

(In this chapter we'll explore creative ways to satisfy this need, such as working part-time or through professional associations and companies that offer policies to individuals and their families.)

_____ 4. You have a successful track record of goal achievement.

(Gerald bought and expanded a retirement community following a successful history of achieving sales goals individually and in sales management in the pharmaceutical industry.)

_____5. You have proven yourself to be self-directed and highly motivated and prefer taking the lead to being supervised.

_____ 6. You are a calculated risk taker with successful risk-taking experience in the past. You do not crave static security.

Do You Have the Right Personal Characteristics to Be an Entrepreneur?

As I interview franchise owners, consultants, and those who have started or purchased businesses, I find one common theme: If you want to play in the entrepreneurial game, you have to be a risk taker. You must be willing to sacrifice the immediate security of consistent income, health insurance, and retirement benefits from an employer for independence, time flexibility, challenge, increased income potential, and greater satisfaction.

When I interviewed Gerald, a multimillionaire owner of a retirement community, he spoke passionately about the development of his business. He said, "As a business owner, you always need to stretch beyond your comfort zone. There is no middle ground; you will either succeed or flop."

Business ownership can be the height of personal expression, but with new business startups having an average five-year survival rate of 33 percent (as reported by the Small Business Administration), they are not for the faint of heart. (Generally speaking, businesses are considered viable if they survive beyond five years.)

If you have experienced involuntary unemployment, you should certainly consider, as one of many options, taking the entrepreneurial route. But first, find out whether you have what it takes to be an entrepreneur. The Small Business Administration offers a free entrepreneur assessment tool, which I highly recommend, at www.sba. gov/assessmenttool/index.html.

After taking the SBA assessment, you will receive a personalized list of additional information/training recommended before you start your business. Steps may include taking free online courses the SBA offers; making a list of questions that are generated by the courses; e-mailing the questions to an online SCORE counselor (a resource partner of the SBA); and then meeting with a business mentor, coach, or counselor to discuss your business needs. If you decide to go ahead with starting or buying a business, you can be coached through the ongoing process.

After teaching several entrepreneurial courses and working with successful entrepreneurs as clients, I have created my personal entrepreneurial assessment, which follows.

Personal Entrepreneurial Characteristics Assessment

Answering the following questions will give you an idea of whether you have the personal characteristics and financial and emotional support system found in many successful entrepreneurs.

1. Are you self-directed, self-motivated, and disciplined in your business activities? ❑ yes ❑ no

2. Do you have strong communication skills and the ability to adapt to different personalities? ❑ yes ❑ no

3. Do you have the physical and emotional stamina to devote long hours to your work? ❑ yes ❑ no

4. Can you obtain financial backing or a loan, or do you have reserves in place to survive a year without income from your business? ❑ yes ❑ no

5. Do you have medical insurance in place or can you obtain this? ❑ yes ❑ no

6. Do you have your family's support in this venture? ❑ yes ❑ no

7. Are you good at planning, organizing, and exercising emotional control? ❑ yes ❑ no

8. Do you have a burning desire to be an entrepreneur, or does entrepreneurship seem to be the only path available? ❑ yes ❑ no

9. Have you researched and found a niche for your business? ❑ yes ❑ no

10. Are you persistent in completing business projects despite delays and setbacks? ❑ yes ❑ no

11. Are you able to survive and adapt to an unpredictable environment? ❑ yes ❑ no

12. Do you have a significant track record of goal achievement? ❑ yes ❑ no

If you answered, "yes" to all these questions, you have what it takes to be an entrepreneur. If you have answered "yes" to at least 10 out of the 12 questions, you can make it as an entrepreneur if you recognize and compensate for the two questions you missed by shoring up your weaknesses.

I have all of my clients who are interested in entrepreneurial activities take this assessment and have found that some clients are over-literal and over-modest about their abilities. No one is perfect. If you can answer *generally* or *usually* to these questions, then you have a definite yes. Don't be too hard on yourself. Cultivate optimism. For example for number 10, I answered "yes." I don't complete all business projects in the time frame I would like to see happen, but I complete all critical A-level business projects on time, such as writing this book and completing clients' resumes and interview practices on time.

The How-to-Fail Guide

You too can be a failed business statistic. Just follow these five simple practices:

- Choose a business that you know nothing about. Your learning curve will be longer and the ride will be more exciting.

- Choose a location that you like because it is convenient to your home; customers will come to you.

- Start with absolutely no capital or reserves. Good things come to those who risk everything (good things like bankruptcy and nervous breakdowns, that is).

- Never ask for professional advice or help. (After all, you can't be a self-made person if anyone helps you.)

- Wing it. Writing a business plan takes too much time and effort.

Congratulations if you have found that you have the financial risk tolerance and general characteristics found in successful entrepreneurs. Fortunately, there are many types of entrepreneurial ventures where the financial risk ranges from moderate to high. If you did not score high on risk tolerance, you can develop greater risk tolerance over time. Read on and find out how.

Exploring Different Kinds of Entrepreneurial Ventures

Fortunately, there are many types of entrepreneurial ventures that range in their risk-taking order from the least financially risky to those involving the most financial risk. In this section we explore the main types of businesses, their associated risk level, and their advantages and disadvantages.

Part-Time Entrepreneurial Employment

Many employers are hiring people on a part-time, project, adjunct, commission, or seasonal basis. Examples are outplacement firms, restaurants, retail operations, mail-delivery stores, and contract and permanent employment firms such as Matrix Resources and Administaff. There is little financial risk in these situations if you recognize the part-time and time-limited potential of these situations. Some of these firms now offer medical insurance for part-time employees. For example, Starbucks offers medical insurance for employees working 20 hours a week. Macy's offers medical insurance for part-time employees willing to work on weekends and some holidays. Matrix Resources offers medical insurance for its contractors. Working in part-time opportunities can provide the medical insurance while you are starting your own business.

Variety Is My Game: Janet Richards, Entrepreneur

Janet began her real-estate career the year before the market plummeted. She loved finding, showing, and closing on homes. She wanted to maintain her license and stay in the business, but she had to find additional income to help support her family. How did she do it? She became a manufacturer's representative for a toy manufacturer. Although she worked on a commission-only basis, the medical benefits were comprehensive. She also imported and sold high-thread-count Egyptian cotton sheet sets.

Janet's advice: Don't put all of your eggs in one basket. Stay aware of moves in the economy and start a savings account.

Table 3.1 takes a look at the advantages and disadvantages of part-time entrepreneurial employment.

Table 3.1: Advantages and Disadvantages of Part-Time Entrepreneurial Employment

Advantages	Disadvantages
Income from multiple streams can be greater than a single corporate position.	Income is inconsistent and unpredictable and you may have to find your own health insurance.
Time can be flexible to accommodate family needs.	Entrepreneurs often work long hours and weekends.
Variety can be enjoyable with no boredom.	Entrepreneurs often feel scattered and pulled in many different directions.
Independence is addictive.	Consultants have inconsistent income and finance their own health and retirement benefits.

Coaching, Consulting, and Training

Coaching, consulting, and training (CCT) requires only a small financial investment to cover business cards and promotional material, including a basic Web site. I would describe the financial risk in consulting, coaching, and training as moderate. You can easily get started on $2,000, but you must be prepared to have no business income for up to six months.

When I first began my business, the largest hurdle was obtaining my first client. Although I had an outstanding corporate career in sales, I had to convince my first client that I would be as exceptional at career consulting and sales training as I was at corporate insurance sales. Fortunately, my first corporate client was well known nationally and paved the way for the next client.

CCT is the most common entrepreneurial option mature career-transition candidates choose. This broad field allows you to tap into expertise that you have developed from past career experiences or develop new expertise in a subject of great personal interest. Startups are usually inexpensive, are relatively free of administrative hassles, and can be implemented quickly.

Table 3.2 takes a look at the advantages and disadvantages of consulting-related business models.

Table 3.2: Advantages and Disadvantages of Coaching, Consulting, and Training

Advantages	Disadvantages
Inexpensive startup costs.	CCTs can make more or less than their corporate salary.
Can be done full- or part-time.	CCTs often work long hours and are never really through with business.
Can be in business quickly.	CCTs usually work solo and do their own marketing and administrative work.
Hours can be flexible.	
Independence is addictive.	CCTs have inconsistent income and must finance their own health and retirement benefits.

Now let's look at two very different solo businesses: a speaking and corporate training business and an image consulting business.

Corporate Speaking and Training: Communication Dynamics

Patty Wood began her corporate training, speaking, and coaching business when she was 22 years old, in conjunction with her career as a college professor in communications. She knew that she had professional presentation talent and was underpaid as an instructor. It was relatively easy for her to transition into professional speaking because she had paid speaking engagements during her career as a college professor.

I met Patty and became a friend when we were both members of the National Speakers Association, and I interviewed her for this book.

We talked about the advantages of time flexibility, a comfortable environment, and no commute working in our home offices. But we both bemoaned the fact that our furry administrative assistants interrupt us by jumping in our laps.

Patti suggests that not only should entrepreneurs have talent and passion for their idea, but they should also prepare a business plan, keep their day job until they are established, and be prudent in controlling expenses.

Making a Fashion Statement Out of Downsizing: Parks Image Group

I first met Peggy Parks when I notified the employees of a major Japanese manufacturing firm that they would be receiving outplacement services. Peggy was their office manager and sales and human resources liaison.

When I first met Peggy, I was initially struck by her fashionable appearance and her vivacity. She had bright, curly auburn hair and was attired in a rust-colored suede skirt and boots. Her makeup and hair were stylish and well done. She didn't fit the stereotype of the somewhat dull and conservatively dressed business manager that I had expected.

As I got to know Peggy better, she confided that she had always loved fashion, and that she considered her downsizing as the perfect opportunity to develop her business as an image consultant. During the time she was in our outplacement services, she attended all of our classes. Peggy read every image book that she could get her hands on, and investigated associations and classes in image consulting. Before she had officially started her own business, she scored her first client by word of mouth at her gym. And, as a result of our conversations, she was kind enough to do makeovers for a number of our career-transition clients attending a career fair.

Peggy is now a well-known certified image consultant. She has also joined the Association of Image Consultants International and is sought after in the Southeast.

Peggy suggests considering a certification if there is one associated with your field of expertise. Certification creates added value in the eye of the buyer and can add to your skills, knowledge, and income.

Buying a Franchise

A franchise is a license that a company (the franchisor) grants to a franchisee to use the company's brand name and its proven systems and procedures to build income and achieve consistency in terms of products and services.

At one time I held the mistaken impression that franchise ownership was not affordable to the average person and that most of the franchises were fast-food restaurants. Not so. After I attended a seminar put on by a well-respected franchise consulting firm, and had two clients and a colleague buy franchises, I learned not only that franchises are affordable, but also that the most popular franchises today include business format franchises such as hairstyling, commercial cleaning, and so on.

The buying and selling of a franchise is highly regulated, so you can do your due diligence on the income potential and know upfront what your financial investment will be. The least expensive franchises allow you to work out of your home or car and include such activities as accounting and tax work, medical transcription, day care, and carpet cleaning. These franchises can cost you from $10,000 to $40,000 and include how-to training and ongoing support. The most expensive franchises are for lodging, restaurants, and fast-food establishments and can cost up to $7M plus. The survival rate of franchises exceeds that of new business startups, but of course varies according to the success of the individual franchise.

Here are some interesting facts about franchises:

- Franchise owners do not want to work for someone else, but they do not want to develop a business from scratch.
- The average franchise costs between $75,000 and $150,000, including franchise and startup fees.
- Franchises have a 50 percent higher success rate than new business startups because they are based on a proven success model.
- Franchises are available in almost every business.

Brightly Burning Franchise: Brightstar Home Care

I interviewed Terry Trace, owner of the Entrepreneur's Source (www.theesource.com/ttrace) in Marietta, Georgia, and asked for his top franchise picks for the next decade. He suggested franchises involving home healthcare, business coaching, education enhancement, and full-service hair salons. These services will always be needed despite economic ups and downs.

Terry shared with me the story of Norman. Norman had sold medical laboratory equipment for 20 years, earning a six-figure-plus income. During a corporate reorganization, he was offered the opportunity to relocate, accept a lesser position, or take a buyout. He took the buyout and decided to explore franchise ownership with Terry.

It took Norman about six weeks to become a franchise owner of Brightstar Home Care. He increased his level of confidence in buying a franchise by attending Discovery Day at two franchises and interviewing successful franchise owners. Learning positive facts helped him overcome his initial fears. He has turned a profit within one year and expects to soon exceed his former salary in medical equipment sales. His business is in keeping with the growing trend in healthcare for people as well as pets.

Terry suggests working with an entrepreneurial consultant and immersing yourself in information about the financial potential of the franchise of interest. Talk with owners of various levels of success and attend a Discovery Day at the home office of the franchise.

Supporting Business: ActionCOACH

Dresden Flynn White was a VP of human resources for 20 years with Kaiser Permanente when she was asked to relocate to California. She opted instead to leave Kaiser to run her own business. Although she did not need to borrow money to buy her ActionCOACH franchise, she believes in borrowing to expand.

Dresden's advice: "I find that most people do not fail because of money, but because they try to do everything themselves and underestimate the need for support in terms of legal, accounting, and business advice."

I was introduced to Dresden by Leslie Kuban of franchise expert Frannet (www.frannet.com). Leslie says that the satisfaction rate is 75 percent in franchise ownership across the board. She says that hair salons, disaster restoration companies, and office-cleaning services remain strong in any economy.

Table 3.3 lays out the advantages and disadvantages of owning a franchise.

Table 3.3: Advantages and Disadvantages of Franchise Ownership

Advantages	Disadvantages
A successful business plan, proven systems, support, and training are provided by the franchisor.	The requirement to work within standardized procedures can frustrate independent types.
Franchises have a higher success rate than new business startups.	Some franchisees feel they do not receive sufficient support.
Franchise prices are fixed and regulated by government disclosure requirements.	Startup costs can be high.
Franchises can be up and running in a relatively short time.	Some successful franchisees resent continuing payments to the franchisor.

Buying a Business

As you explore the possibility of buying an existing business, the stakes and the risk involved can increase dramatically because of the costs involved in buying a business, the lack of structured ongoing support, and the volatility of the economy.

Having interviewed business owners and brokers, I found that their advice involving flourishing businesses often mirrored that of the franchise brokers and was centered around eldercare, commercial cleaning businesses that thrive in all times, and businesses that thrive in times of economic depression such as dollar stores. Also, consider businesses that are "green" (or environmentally centered), because their clients often receive tax incentives for buying. Despite the risk involved in buying a business, the financial gains can be outstanding. And based on my research, whereas many businesses cost over $1 million, there are those to be had for as little as $59,000.

Retirement Community Tycoon: Sugar Creek Development Corporation

Gerald Dominick had a successful career as a district sales manager for Baxter Pharmaceuticals but had always wanted to own his own business. I asked him whether this was the American dream. He said that he didn't know about it being everyone's dream, but he remembered his mother admiring people who owned their own business, and it was his dream.

Gerald stumbled upon the opportunity to buy a retirement community with manufactured homes. A friend partnered with him, and he left the comfort and security of his corporate career for the precipice of business ownership, where he would either summit or plummet.

I asked him about the financials of buying a business. Did he hire a CPA or go to great extent to make sure the business was well valued? "No," he said. Their first business plan was written on a cocktail napkin. But the land in the retirement community had intrinsic value, and they were able to borrow the money they needed to buy it and develop it. The borrowing was in the millions. "You will succeed if there is no safety blanket," he said. He had to pay his notes as they came due, and he did not have a year's reserve in the bank. But he did have the support of a loving family.

Eventually Gerald bought out his partner and the park of 30 spaces now has 195 spaces. He is incredibly financially successful and is considering selling the business, despite the fact that he has no day-to-day management responsibility.

Advice from Gerald: Make sure to have the support of your family. Don't be afraid of taking a calculated risk. Having great people skills and self-confidence helps.

Table 3.4 takes a realistic look at some of the advantages and disadvantages of buying a business.

Table 3.4: Advantages and Disadvantages of Buying a Business

Advantages	Disadvantages
Not limited to franchise business.	No organized buying market.
Business can be running well and be profitable.	No standard financial disclosure requirements.
Owner can participate as much as desired.	Financing is difficult unless new owner has experience or there is intrinsic value to business.
Enormous income potential.	Transaction costs are higher and time to close longer than with franchises.
Freedom to operate.	No formal support mechanism.
No ongoing franchise fees.	

Starting Your Own Business

You can see from the entrepreneurial options we have covered that when someone expresses the desire to start their own business, they may mean franchise ownership, consulting, or buying a business. And then there is the option of starting your own new business.

Starting your own business from scratch can be the most difficult and risky entrepreneurial venture, because you have no model to follow of proven systems and procedures. The failure rate is high—some sources claim between 50 and 77 percent. And you often have no intrinsic value of land, buildings, or equipment to put up as collateral. But starting your own business can be a satisfying and lucrative business model.

The Story of Video Impact: Richard Hunter

I have been a customer of Video Impact for 10 years, so it was logical that I would interview the founder, Richard Hunter, about starting a business from scratch, growing a successful business, and multiplying the business.

Richard began his business when he was 46 years old after working for Marriott hotels for a number of years as the director of training.

Working in training, Richard recognized that finding quality video production and editing was difficult. He determined that he would have little competition in providing quality and accessible service. He opened his first Video Impact store with one employee, without borrowing any money. He was profitable in less than a year and has opened multiple stores in Southern states that he has sold profitably. When DVD replaced video, Video Impact became known for transferring video and movies to DVD, and for skillful editing and duplication.

Advice from Richard: The advantage of having your own business is that there is no insecurity from corporate politics. If you don't like your business, you can fire yourself. You have time flexibility and can make an excellent income. Choose a business that you think is fun and that you are passionate about so that you enjoy going to work. Richard says that as far as he is concerned, there are no disadvantages to starting a business.

Table 3.5 lists the major advantages and disadvantages of starting your own business.

Table 3.5: Advantages and Disadvantages of Starting Your Own Business

Advantages	Disadvantages
Self-actualization, the opportunity to develop your "big idea" and do it your way.	You are developing your own business model from scratch.
Startups offer the possibility of large business returns.	Startups offer significant risk and are often difficult to finance.
Your business has future value to expand, to franchise, and to sell.	Startups often consume an excessive commitment of time and energy.
Some businesses are profitable in less than one year.	Financial success can take a number of years.

Deciding on a Legal Business Entity

Clients frequently ask me whether they should form a sole proprietorship, Chapter C, Chapter S, or LLC. The following sections offer helpful information on which legal-entity type of business is appropriate for you.

Sole Proprietorship

Sole proprietorship (ownership) is quick, uncomplicated, and inexpensive. There are no documents to file with the state, but you may need a license if required by the state. There are many positives to this business model. There are no legal startup costs and little administration, with the main negatives being that the owner's personal assets may be used to pay back business debt, and your liability is unlimited.

I have always had a sole proprietorship and have no business debt or legal liability issues, so this has been a good model for me. If you are a sole proprietor, you are the only owner, but you can have a business with multiple streams of income, such as training, consulting, writing, and so on.

Bill Elemeyer, a senior vice president with well-known outplacement firm Lee Hecht Harrison, was interviewed in the *Orange County Register*. He describes his own business as career transition, executive coaching, professional speaking, and marketing consulting. Bill expressed the belief that people with solid work experience should be able to sculpt their skills into a solid portfolio of self-employment.

General Partnerships

General partnerships share most of the pluses and minuses of sole proprietorship. On the plus side, two or more owners share business responsibilities. On the minus side, all partners are responsible for debts and business-related actions of the other partners, and they share unlimited liability. Therefore, it is very important that detailed partnership agreements are drawn up to clarify as many liability and responsibility issues as possible before the business is in place.

Corporations

There are three types of corporations: C, S, and LLC. Table 3.6 details the basic differences that you should investigate in detail before making a choice.

Table 3.6: Differences Among Corporation Types

Corp. Type	Ownership	Type of Entity	Main Advantages	Main Disadvantages	Taxes
Subchapter C	Unlimited shareholders	Separate legal entity	Limited liability; company-paid fringe benefits; capital easy to raise through stock sale	Costly to form; administrative duties; taxation on corporate earnings and individual dividends	Corporation pays its own
Subchapter S	Limited to 35 shareholders	Separate legal entity	Limited liability; no double taxation—shareholders report income on individual tax returns	Costly to form; administrative duties	Paid by owner(s)
LLC	Owned by members	Separate legal entity	Limited liability; no double taxation; less paperwork	Ownership hard to transfer	Taxed as partnership or corporation

My career clients frequently ask me about setting up a corporation even before they have a "big idea" envisioned or a business plan in place. I believe that you should not do business until you have established the legal structure of your new organization, but it is folly to agonize over the business structure before you have a big idea and a business plan in place.

Also, continue to ask yourself whether you have the personal characteristics and support to be an entrepreneur. If you do, continue your exploration and get started.

How Does Entrepreneurship Fit in with Future Employment Trends?

Those of us in outplacement, staffing, and recruiting have seen the shift from full-time employment to project, part-time employment and consulting opportunities. Corporations continue to operate more leanly in order to be internationally competitive, with the average job length being two years. So if you are interested in entrepreneurship but need help in increasing your ability to take financial risk, follow the advice in the following sidebar.

Three Ways to Increase Your Ability to Take Employment and Financial Risk

- Take one small step: Go to www.google.com and identify the top three growth industries for the next 10 years. How could you participate in their growth by being a contractor, a consultant, a franchise owner, or a business owner? If healthcare is the number-one industry, could you work or consult in a healthcare environment? Could you start a healthcare-related business or buy a healthcare franchise?

- Decide on a product you like and find out how you can purchase it on a wholesale basis and sell it on a retail basis. For example, Janet Richards, an entrepreneur, is a reseller of cotton sheets. She and her business partner found these sheets by researching "cotton sheets" on Google. They are selling them to groups for fund-raising purposes. They will soon add duvets to their offerings.

- Go to an entrepreneurial business fair and investigate one or more business opportunities. Use Google to find a fair in your area featuring businesses that might interest you.

After you identify which businesses interest you, use the worksheet below to clarify your ideas.

Business Exploration Worksheet

I. Make a list of the types of businesses that interest you.

_____

_____

_____

2. Explore franchise opportunities in these businesses.

3. Look at these businesses for sale on the Internet or through a business broker.

4. Consider opportunities to consult or have your own business. What is your area of interest or expertise?

_____

_____

_____

5. In what areas could you do part-time work to develop your entrepreneurial interest and increase your income?

_____

_____

_____

As you can see from these wonderful entrepreneurial examples, you may have the resources to buy a multimillion-dollar business or you may need to start small with an Internet store selling your favorite products. Some people dive right in and plan their business on a cocktail napkin. Others spend months in due diligence and investigation.

There is no right or wrong way to get started as an entrepreneur. It's just important to get started—to make your dream a reality. And don't let your age get in the way of your success.

CHAPTER 4

Designing a Career That Mirrors Your Passions, Interests, and Abilities

The good news about a second career or next career is that you have learned from experience what you don't want to do next.

Changing careers is easier for people who crave adventure and variety, and more difficult for those who prefer lifestyle stability. In fact, some people have been forced into designing a new career because of unexpected circumstances such as divorce, age, corporate downsizing, or changing economic conditions. But regardless of why you are designing a new career, you have the benefit of your past experience—not only in the lessons learned, but in what we call transferable experience. For example, sales and customer service skills are easily transferred from one industry to another, as are good computer skills. Thus, a customer service representative with good computer skills can become an administrative assistant or an inside sales professional with minor additional training.

Designing a second or next career allows you to build a career that mirrors your passions, interests, and abilities.

Look at Your Past Experience for Clues

Let's have a little fun as we get started. In a minute I'm going to ask you to list in the following worksheet the part-time jobs and full-time jobs you have held and what you've learned from these experiences in terms of life lessons and skills. Here is my own list to prime your pump. I have boldfaced my lessons learned and skills and abilities.

1. Harris Printing Company: I assembled print material by hand one summer in high school. I learned that I was **reliable** and **punctual** and **enjoyed making money.** I learned that I **do not enjoy the routine work** of an assembly line.

2. Rich's (Macy's) Department Store: During the holidays and summers in college and when I was teaching school, I was a contingent salesperson. I sold in all departments. I found I was good in **sales** but disliked the down time of personal sales.

3. Southern Engineering Company: I did minor drafting, such as coloring electrical transformers on maps, the summer before college. I learned that I **hated routine work.** I learned I **enjoyed people more than tasks.**

4. Decatur High School, Kings Mt. High School: As a high school teacher, I thoroughly **enjoyed my students** and **liked being in charge** of my classroom. I **didn't like being micromanaged** by one principal. The **salary** was **not sufficient** and I wanted more **challenge.**

5. Allstate Insurance Company and several other insurance companies: I enjoyed claims adjusting at first, especially when I **investigated claims out of the office. I hated the containment of being in the office.** I wanted **more money** and **more authority.**

6. Alexsis, Alexander & Alexander, The Aon Group: I **disliked administrative work** and as a corporate attorney I had **too much paperwork, down time,** and lack of **people contact.** I loved being **top sales person** internationally and being the western division sales manager. I had enough **autonomy, people contact,** and a **forum to excel** in terms of **promotion** and **money.**

7. Atlanta Career Transition: I love having my own business as a career consultant. I have an opportunity to assist in the success of a **wide variety of clients.** I enjoy **presenting** workshops and corporate seminars. There is very little I don't like about what I do. I am **never bored.** I have plenty of **challenge** and an opportunity to **make good money.** I am a published **author.** I need a personal assistant to handle my **administrative work** and **personal errands.** I need **more free time** and to **give up routine work.**

8. What's next? I will always have Atlanta Career Transition, but I may receive additional legal training in employment law as an add-on service to my clients. I am also interested in a degree in counseling to further serve my clients and their families. I will hire a personal assistant a few days a week.

You can see from an analysis of my past part-time and full-time work a career progression that helped me learn about my passions, interests, and abilities. My work passions are counseling people, writing books, and presenting. My abilities include sales, sales management, corporate law, writing, corporate training and presenting, and career counseling.

Now let's take a look at your past experience. Include both part-time and full-time positions. Write a short paragraph about each position describing your likes and dislikes about each position and the skills and abilities you learned and/or used while working in these positions. Boldface or underline these.

What I Have Learned in All of My Past Career Experiences

1. _____

_____

_____

2. _____

_____

_____

3. _____

_____

_____

4. _____

_____

_____

5. _____

_____

_____

(continued)

(continued)

6. _____

_____

_____

7. _____

_____

_____

8. _____

_____

_____

As you can see, it helps to know what you do well and enjoy and what you absolutely detest. Now, I'll show you what I do next with my clients to assist them in designing a career that mirrors their passions, interests, and abilities.

The Career Change Counseling Process

Usually, I meet people interested in changing careers first over the telephone. My prospective clients have heard of me through a satisfied client, my book, my Web site in an internet search, a magazine article, or a speaking engagement. When we first talk I ask them to send me a copy of their resume so that I can review their past experience before giving career guidance. Past experience is an excellent talking point.

If the prospect is undecided about what's next, I recommend that they take a formal career assessment. I lean toward the BirkmanDirect, which I detailed in chapter 2. I also like the Myers-Briggs assessment. When individuals agree to let me become their career counselor, I have them take the BirkmanDirect or Myers-Briggs assessment online. Next we set up a two-hour personal or telephone meeting (if they are out of town or overseas) to interpret the results. The following sidebar is an example of the fascinating details that can come out in a two-hour meeting and how my clients decide on their future career paths.

A Two-Hour Career Choice Meeting

"Hi Kecia, were you able to find my office easily?" I asked.

"Yes, I got a GPS for Christmas and it really helps. Does your club stamp my parking ticket?" I assured Kecia that we would get her ticket stamped when we took a break.

"I'm quite excited about the results of your Birkman; you have many career options to consider," I said.

Kecia and I started through the entire document, covering first her strengths and needs; next, a lifestyle grid showing her usual style of behavior, and what happens to her under stress. Finally, we came to her suggested job families and job titles. I noticed that her excitement was building.

"Look at all of your career choices, from careers in science such as a medical technician to a research engineer. Plus you also have many opportunities in the employee relations category, including teaching and becoming a paralegal."

Kecia responded, "I am overwhelmed. I am interested in what it takes to be a paralegal. How long is the training? What does it cost? I'm also interested in knowing more about being an environmental specialist. I have done so much work in library research that I am ready for a change."

I explained to Kecia that I would e-mail her the BirkmanDirect results that day after our meeting and that she should click on the blue links into the Bureau of Labor Statistics's *Occupational Outlook Handbook* to research careers as a paralegal and an environmental specialist.

Also, if possible, she should set up an information interview with someone working in these two careers. (Details about conducting an information interview are covered in chapter 2.) I gave her the number of a former client who was working as a paralegal and told her to look up environmental specialists in Atlanta and call to see whether she could set up an information interview. We agreed on a check-in time in a week for Kecia to report to me her findings. After that, we would work toward a career decision.

Kecia called me a week later with her homework complete.

"I have decided to become a paralegal. My background in research will help and I can obtain my studies from an online university, take a test, and be certified in six months. They also offer help in placement. Also, the profession of paralegal has a projected 22 percent growth rate from 2006 to 2016, much higher than average. Talking to

(continued)

(continued)

Judy, your paralegal client, really solidified my choice. She said that I would have an advantage with my previous work experience. And she loves what's she's doing."

"That's just great," I offered. "Shall we put our three-month program on hold while you finish your course, and then I'll help you design a resume that reflects your past experience and your new training as a paralegal?" We put her resume and further advice on hold and did just that. Eight months later Kecia was employed as a paralegal.

As a usual practice, my clients don't decide on an entirely new career in a week. The average time to make the decision to follow a new career path is about four to six months. But once they make the commitment to go back to school for six weeks or up to two years, they are hooked on the new career.

To date, I have seen a success rate of 75 percent in dramatic career change with my clients, which may turn into 100 percent. Clients that have become medical technicians and private investigators have succeeded in reemployment. A client who became an attorney after a very successful career in healthcare administration is stuck in an employment recession, but I honestly believe her Juris Doctorate degree will pay off. Until then she can fall back on career number one. It is always smart to take a career assessment and do your homework before signing up for additional education and expense.

On the other hand, there are those of us who are spontaneous. We have to get our hands wet and try on a new profession. This is me. I took a quarter of interior design work, which was very time-consuming and expensive, only to learn that I would be lucky to start a career in interior design at $24,000 a year. Of course, this decision was prior to becoming a career counselor, and at the time I had a six-figure income. I literally spent as much time on interior design homework as law school homework. I have great respect for interior designers. Their curriculum has much in common with architects and is quite challenging.

Time-Tested Steps to Discover Your Passions, Interests, and Abilities and Advance to Your Next Career

Here are the steps I recommend for discovering the next career that's right for you.

Find a Career Counselor

Get professional help from a career counselor, through Crossroads Career Network (www.crossroadscareer.org), or through your state's workforce development office. To find your nearest One-Stop career center, visit America's Service Locator online at www. servicelocator.org. Type your ZIP code or city name and click the Search button.

Changing careers is both easier and faster with professional support. If you have been downsized, you may be able to obtain a grant for educational expenses from your local workforce development office.

Define and Explore Your Career Options

Take a career assessment and then explore careers that interest you at www.bls.gov/oco to determine growth potential, salary, and educational requirements. Career titles are presented in alphabetical order within job type groups with extensive descriptive information. Ask yourself the following questions:

- How do these career options align with your passions and interests in terms of how you spend your spare time and discretionary money?
- How do these career options align with your transferable past experience?
- How do these career options reflect activities that you enjoy and deemphasize things that you don't enjoy?

After taking a career assessment, most individuals will investigate two or three career options further or simply reaffirm that their strengths, interests, and abilities continue to lie in their current position, although they may be willing to change companies.

Set Up Information Interviews

Conduct information interviews with individuals working in positions that interest you. Get advice on the preferred courses, schools, and companies that are hiring. Have your list of prepared questions as outlined in chapter 2.

Get Hands-on Experience

Consider being an intern or an apprentice, not only to practice what you know or learn a new skill, but to determine whether this is the right position for you. Don't let your age deter you from asking for an internship or an apprenticeship opportunity. If you have discretionary income, you might want to check out Vocation Vacations (www.vocationvacations.com), where you pay for being personally mentored and shadow the mentor in an actual work environment.

Make Your Choice

Make an informed career choice after you have thoroughly researched your careers of interest. If you have comprehensive information and still feel undecided about your choice, take a look at your new career choice using both a left-brain (logical) and a right-brain (feeling) perspective.

First, write down the characteristics of your ideal job, which can include base salary, bonus, car allowance, commute, coworkers, and so on. Then rate your new career option against an additional option or as compared to your current position. Use 5 as your highest characteristic score. Here is an example of what a chart comparison looks like.

	Real-Estate Attorney	Human Resource Professional
Salary	5	4
Enjoyment	3	5
Security	2	4
Commute	2	4
Total Score	12	17

In this example, the former career is as a real-estate attorney and the new option is as an HR professional using legal background but with new HR training. The HR professional position wins point wise from a left-brain perspective. But to get the right-brain perspective, try flipping a coin to get in tune with your feelings. Name each side of the coin with your choices and then literally flip the coin. If you are delighted or disappointed with the results, you are in touch with your gut feelings about this decision. In this case, the HR position also won on the coin flip.

At one point in my career in sales, my former manager, then CEO of a growing company in Florida, asked me to interview for a sales management position at his company. My husband and I flew down to look over the town and for me to discuss my potential position. The salary and bonus potential were outstanding and I knew that I could work successfully with the CEO. My husband was willing to move, but I knew without flipping my coin that my ties to Atlanta were too strong for me to move to a much smaller city with few cultural activities. If the offer had been here, I would have accepted it.

Consider Your Career Design Options

After you have made your career choice, be flexible in considering how this career can play out in full-time, part-time, and self-employment options. For example, I am a self-employed career counselor, but I could also be a permanently employed career counselor for an outplacement firm, corporation, or college. I can also be self-employed and work part-time for an outplacement firm, corporation, or college. Remember that future employment trends are not leaning toward permanent employment. Many of my clients indicate in their cover letters that they are open for both permanent and contract positions.

Write Your Resume

Prepare a professional resume or CV (curriculum vitae, a narrative version of the resume) directed toward your new career objective. Make sure that you have designed a resume showing your transferable skills from former positions and that the new resume is a very close match to the new position. You will need a traditional resume and a text-only resume for posting online. In chapter 5, you'll find examples and how-to details for both types of resumes.

Write Other Promotional Material

If you elect to go the self-employed or partially employed route, you'll want to read chapter 6, which covers other promotional material to start your entrepreneurial venture.

Market Yourself

Now it's up to you to aggressively market yourself. Network, answer online and newspaper ads, go to job fairs, post your profile on LinkedIn, contact recruiters, and do a strategic mailing of your resume to potential employers. Leave no stone unturned. The more aggressive you are, the quicker you will be employed.

Case Study: Dan Ogletree

Dan Ogletree co-owned a printing company with his dad and his brother. After the death of his dad, the need for professionally print-ed documents declined and Dan and his brother closed their shop. Dan visited me after taking a temporary job as a warehouse foreman. He asked me for help in answering the question, "What's next?" He had never had a formal resume. Although he had trained to be an electrician after high school, he never worked in the field, because his father persuaded him to join the family printing company. So he was willing to start from scratch in his mid-fifties.

Dan opted to take a Myers-Briggs career assessment. Of his suggested options, he was most intrigued by the position of private investiga-tor. I asked him to research this career by scheduling an information interview with one of my contacts who was a private investigator and to locate a convenient community college offering a certification as a private investigator.

Right after we started working together, Dan took a previously booked cruise and attended to other family responsibilities. So it was at least six months before he took the course as a private investigator. Then, not by chance, he became a star student and made friends with the instructor, who gave him a job lead after graduation.

I had to prepare Dan's new private investigation resume post haste. Dan is now happily employed by the largest private investigation firm in the state, dealing primarily with insurance fraud. He is start-ing with a reasonable per diem rate, which will rise when he has more experience.

Tip: When you are taking classes as part of your career retooling, it pays to make friends with the course instructor. That person probably has job leads and good networking contacts.

Looking at Stumbling Blocks

Once you've found something you want to do, you might start coming up with all the reasons why it's not feasible for you. Here's a look at the most common stumbling blocks and how you can get around them.

I Can't Afford to Go Back to School for Continuing Education

You might be thinking, "I can't afford to go back to school," before investigating the cost of the education, the time involved, or how it might be financed. Some continuing-education studies can be done in a week, or at the most, six weeks. Other associate degrees can take two years. Most people who go back for continuing education do it while they are working by taking courses at night, on weekends, or online. Dan completed his course as a private investigator in six weeks. Many continuing-education courses offering certification fall between $500 and $1,000. In some cases, workforce development centers and One-Stop centers can help you secure career development funding. In other cases, new careers might offer on-the-job training, or you might want to try an internship or apprenticeship.

I Can't Make Enough Money from My Passions and Interests

A psychologist friend of mind said to look beyond the outward appearance to the essence of what you enjoy in terms of your passions and interests. For example, a budding abstract artist friend says that he will not be able to make a career except as a starving artist. The budding artist can keep painting, showing and selling in galleries and on his Web site, and learning in coursework how to identify and appraise fine art, jewelry, and furniture. Many of today's appraisers do not work for companies, but are self-employed and also make money buying and selling.

I'm Afraid of Making a Mistake

If you don't invest too much money or time, you can afford to make a mistake. But the worst mistake you can make is not to take a step in the direction of your dreams.

When we were growing up, my brothers and I heard my parents bemoaning their lack of money and career advancement. My dad would say, "If only I had gone back to school after the war on the

GI Bill and finished my electrical engineering degree. But I don't see how I could have done this and traveled on my engineering job. Plus, we had started our family." Then my mother would add, "I wish that you had gotten that manager's job at that local REA office. We would have both enjoyed living in Aiken, South Carolina. I wonder if not having the degree hurt you."

Neal, Rich, and I had a little act we played that mimicked our parents' "what-if" conversations. We pretended to rock on a front porch. We were in our eighties and bemoaned all the things we wished we had done in our careers. Consequently, my parents' lack of adventure spawned two entrepreneurs out of the three of us. Neal worked as a court reporter, but Rich and I have been self-employed for many years. Our parents never saw or heard our act because we respected them too much and wanted to continue living at home and eating mom's good food.

I encourage you to take a step in the direction of expressing your passions and interests in your second or next career. Compare what you have to gain with what you have to lose.

CHAPTER 5

Acquire Inexpensive Skill and Credential Updates

As a mature worker, your career transition shares a common thread with that of a recent high school or college graduate in that you too may be asking yourself, "What do I want to do for the rest of my life?" or "What's next?" But here the similarity ends. You hold the trump card because of your work experience and life wisdom.

Voluntary or involuntary career transition is an opportunity for you to choose the work you love and then to update or acquire the required skills and credentials to be gainfully employed. Based on my experience as a career counselor, the majority of my clients do not want to go back to school for a four-year degree or take out a home-equity loan to pay for additional education, but they are very open to inexpensive skill and credential updates that do not take a lot of time.

"When love and skill work together, expect a masterpiece."

–John Ruskin

In creating a next career for yourself, you can choose to stay in the same position within a different industry, take a different position within the same industry, or make a complete change by seeking a different position within a different industry. This chapter looks at skill and credential updates you can get to help you reach all of these choices.

Getting the Information You Need

One of the negative stereotypes some employers hold is that experienced workers have stale skills and credentials. To avoid reinforcing that negative stereotype, you need to do some research—regardless of the type of career move you choose.

Let Your Fingers Do the Walking

To check out certification, training, and education requirements; salary range; and the future employment outlook for a familiar or unfamiliar job position, begin by using the Web. These two resources can provide you with information without the time, effort, and expense of setting up appointments with people, getting dressed for a meeting, or traveling:

- **Simply Hired:** To obtain a job description; education, certification, and experience requirements; and median salary, go to www.simplyhired.com and fill in the name of the position under Keywords. I tried a difficult one: hedge fund assistant. I was pleased to discover many open position descriptions. I didn't fill in the city of interest because my client was open to relocation, but I definitely noticed that these positions are predominantly in New York, where the mean salary is $63,000. (If you find no open positions in your area, this does not mean that there are no open positions, but it does throw up a red flag that there are either no current open positions or that you will need to uncover them through networking.) I found that education requirements included a bachelor's degree with an average of two to five years of experience. Simply Hired does not address the future employment outlook.

- *Occupational Outlook Handbook:* Also, use the Bureau of Labor Statistics's *Occupational Outlook Handbook* (www. bls.gov/oco) to research careers. You will not find current job openings, but you can determine all other needed information, including the future employment outlook. I searched for "paralegal" and found that an associate or bachelor's degree is usually required, but a legal assistant will be considered; and that a paralegal certificate is preferred. The outlook is excellent for the position, with a mean salary of $33,920 to $54,690.

Costs and times of credential updates vary widely. Check several sources. Ask for recommendations. Also, there are possibilities for paid internships while you are getting certified. Look for training information in the *Occupational Outlook Handbook* and consult with an individual working in your field of interest for a recommendation.

Start Doing Some Talking

Regardless of whether you are seeking a different position within a familiar industry, looking for the same position in an unfamiliar industry, or following the entrepreneurial route, you can embrace the change more gracefully if you follow these suggestions:

- Conduct information interviews with people in the type of position that interests you.

- Consider working in your position of interest as an assistant, apprentice, intern, or volunteer. In a search engine, type the words *internship, apprentice,* or *volunteer opportunities* and your area or location of interest. You'll be amazed at the number of existing opportunities you'll discover. You may even be able to create your own opportunity during an information interview.

  The difference between an apprentice and an intern is that an apprentice exchanges labor for instruction and experience and is paid as he learns. An intern exchanges labor for experience but is supposed to have basic skills in the position and industry. Internships may be either paid or unpaid.

- Consider working in the position on a temporary or part-time basis. Look for opportunities through temporary employment agencies, which often offer free training in computer skills. Many temporary positions develop into permanent jobs.

Get your feet wet before you make a decision. You will have much more confidence in yourself and your decision if you invest as much time as necessary (or you can afford) in researching your options.

> ### How to Conduct an Information Interview
>
> - Make a personal or telephone appointment at the person's convenience. Make it clear that you are looking for information and not asking for a job.
>
> - Be considerate of the other person's time and be well prepared with your questions.
>
> - Ask about experience, educational and credential requirements, and salary range.
>
> - Inquire about hours and conditions of employment, including hiring, future growth potential, and assistant or internship possibilities.
>
> - Start with small talk to keep the interview from sounding like an interrogation.
>
> - Make sure that you have your resume and business card with you—just in case you have an opportunity to share them or are asked for them.
>
> - Send a thank-you note after the information interview.

Rethink the Money

Many of the positions you investigate may be low paying compared to your previous salary. You may find yourself asking, "Why would anyone in their right mind work for this low salary or hourly rate?" There are a number of positive reasons why people accept lower wages. Those reasons include

- Time flexibility
- The freedom to hold concurrent (multiple) positions
- The desire to no longer work full-time for "the man"
- The ability to express interests and values, to be challenged, and so on
- The chance to do what you've always wanted to do
- The opportunity to learn and progress in a new position or industry and make even more money

Of all the reasons mature workers give for choosing low-paying positions, make sure that yours is not one forced on you by default. Don't allow yourself to be no longer marketable in your field. Don't refuse to take the time or expense to update your skills and credentials. Take control of your future by using your wisdom and experience to make wise choices today.

Refresh Your Skills and Credentials for the Same Position

When you are seeking a different position in the same industry, the same position in a different industry, or starting an entrepreneurial venture, you may not need to update your credentials. If you have kept up your licensure, retained memberships, taken recent continuing-education courses, had current on-the-job training, or recently attended a college or university, you may be good to go.

On the other hand, if you have had no skills or credential updates since high school or college, you will usually need to update them. Updating skills and credentials demonstrates a clear career commitment and does not have to be a costly, extremely time-consuming experience.

Gina was a Human Resources Director for a major governmental agency. When she was 52 years old, she took an "early out," accepting a reduced early retirement salary to pursue her passion, contract training for corporations and seminar companies. After five years of inconsistent training income, excessive travel, tired feet, and a declining IRA, Gina opted to reenter the field of human resources. However, she had let her Senior Professional in Human Resources (SPHR) credentials expire and had to take a test to reinstate them.

Now happily situated in a senior human resources position, Gina has no regrets about the five years she spent pursuing her passion. She is remaining flexible as her future unfolds. Gina reminds us all that passions and ideal careers change as life circumstances change.

Think Before You Let a License Expire

When you are leaving a position where you are currently licensed, you should seriously consider maintaining your license and memberships at your own expense. You may want to use them in the future. Although I do not actively practice law, I maintain my license on an inactive status. If I were to drop my licensure, I would have to take the grueling bar exam again before I could practive law.

Here are a few examples of job seekers who updated their skills and credentials for the same position in the same or different industry. Notice that some cases do not require formal recertification or training. Salary figures are taken from Salary.com, Indeed, and the *Occupational Outlook Handbook*.

Table 5.1: Updating Skills and Credentials for the Same Position

Position	Skill and Credential Updates	Update Cost and Time	Salary Potential
Human Resource Professional in manufacturing: updating credentials, reentering the workforce (healthcare)	Take PHR or SPHR test for human resources certification or recertification	Certification preparation courses and test; course is $1,295 for SHRM members; certification test is $250–$375; three days	Depending on the position, level, and location, mean salary $32,500–$47,600
Customer service representative in telecommunications to customer service representative for printer manufacturer (business-to-business services)	Rely on transferable credentials and experience; learn current industry news, trends, and buzzwords in your research; use these in your resume and interview	N/A	$33,600–$44,600

Refresh Your Skills and Credentials for a Different Position

The transition from one position to another in the same industry is not always a matter of skill or credential updates. Transitioning often involves convincing senior management that you are ready for a position of increasing responsibility, or may require moving to another company where you have not been previously stereotyped. You may have heard the definition of an expert: someone who is from out of town. Here's a case study of someone who made the transition.

Case Study

I entered the insurance brokerage industry with the position title administrative assistant. I had a college degree, a law degree, and years of supervisory work experience, but I was an unproven commodity in a startup subsidiary of a major corporation.

After a year, I mentioned to our senior vice president that I was interested in a management position. His immediate response was, "What makes you think you have management potential?" And, "I already have enough stallions in this organization." I was devastated.

The senior VP saw me through the lens of my original position. I reminded him of my supervisory experience—and my graduation from law school, cum laude, while working full-time—but this was not enough to change his mind.

I continued to accept and request challenging assignments and submit original ideas. Less than a year later, the senior vice president sent me on two difficult and highly visible assignments: to start an office in Miami and to rescue a troubled office in L.A. Dramatic results brought promotions to vice president and senior vice president, and salary increases followed.

You too can change senior management's perception. Here's how:

- Make your desires known.
- Persistently demonstrate your talent, commitment, and new ideas.
- Volunteer for challenging and visible assignments.
- Perform effectively in temporary management positions.

Refresh Your Skills and Earn Credentials in a Different Industry

Jana had a successful pharmaceutical sales management career following a successful career as a pharmaceutical sales representative. After a major downsizing event, Jana sought to establish herself as an executive healthcare recruiter. Although she had successful placements, she discovered that the unpredictability of her income would not support her family. However, this on-the-job training experience along with her sales management experience in pharmaceuticals qualified her to be sought after by a medical staffing recruiter. After six months, she is happily settled in and productive.

There are many reasons why you may want or need to change industries. Like Jana, you may find that changes in the economy have caused your former industry to be financially unhealthy and not hiring. Your position may have been rendered obsolete through advances in automation. Or you may no longer be interested in your former position or former industry for your own reasons: interest, values, and so on. You may be ready to seek a different position in a different, thriving industry such as healthcare.

Table 5.2: Updating Skills and Credentials: Different Position, Different Industry

Position	Skill and Credential Updates	Update Cost and Time	Salary Potential
Sales manager from sales professional in office supply business (business-to-business services)	Use functional resume to illustrate leadership experience; take sales management seminar—many are industry specific	Sales management seminar: $1,800; two days	$124,978–$176,624
Former corporate attorney becomes an eldercare attorney (services for the aging population)	Activate status in state bar association; take continuing-education courses in estate planning	$1,000 to reactivate status and take continuing legal education courses (approximately $200 per course)	$94,700–$153,684, depending on employment status
Human resource professional with master's degree leaves IT field to become online professor (education)	Five years of experience and advanced degree	N/A	$43,000 full time

Acquiring Skills and Credentials for an Entirely New Career

Life really gets interesting when you choose your career transition time to create an entirely new identity for yourself. You will be wise to be aware of the shortlist of industries and positions suggested by the Bureau of Labor Statistics and as indicated by outplacement firms, employment agencies, and recruiting firms.

In chapter 1, "Making Future Employment Trends Work for You," I covered the growing trend of nonpermanent employment and entrepreneurial ventures. This means that when you are creating an entirely new identity, you should seriously consider permanent and nonpermanent employment in the industries discussed in this section.

As this book is going to press, the top industries predicted by the Bureau of Labor Statistics to surge ahead until 2016 are in management; scientific and technical consulting services; employment services; healthcare; education; local government; and computer systems design and related services. Industries and positions in recent decline involve banking, real estate, construction, and manufacturing, especially automotive and retail. These declines have affected employment numbers in many other industry sectors.

It's up to you to stay current with employment trends, not only by visiting the Bureau of Labor Statistics Web site (www.bls.gov), but also by reading your local newspaper and keeping up with local and national employment news. When you are considering employment or self-employment in a specific occupation, look at the *Occupational Outlook Handbook* at the BLS Web site for employment outlook. Also look on SimplyHired to see the number of openings advertised.

As you investigate position requirements in these industries, you may be surprised at the low cost and short training time involved in preparing yourself for a new career. To show skill and credential updates and income potential, I have selected a few representative examples from three industries with strong future employment growth.

Careers in Healthcare

Healthcare is one of the industries offering the greatest potential employment growth in the U.S. labor force. You can confirm this informally by looking at the employment ads in your weekend paper. Healthcare needs of the large baby-boomer-and-beyond generations are creating a labor shortage that later generations cannot supply because they are fewer in number.

Table 5.3 presents selected positions in healthcare with information on skill and credential updates and income potential.

Table 5.3: Examples of Healthcare Career Updates

Position	Skill and Credential Updates	Update Cost and Time	Salary Potential
Medical coder	Certificate in medical coding	$60 online; four months	$36,725–$45,856
Nursing home administrator	BA or BS degree and certification; or Administrator in Training Program: after one year, assistant or interim administrator	Six months to four years	Median $72,523 with experience
Radiologic technician	Certificate or associate degree	Costs vary; one to four years	$42,800–$51,300
Geriatric social worker/geriatric professional	BS degree in social work; certificate or CEUs in aging, or background in healthcare	$500	$32,590–$55,000

Healthcare Notes

Make a note of any of these careers or other healthcare careers that interest you. Do your research and plan an information interview with someone working in the field.

_____

_____

_____

_____

Careers in Education and Educational Services

In looking at careers in education, you may think only of teaching. But looking at the Web site of a school system, college, university, or continuing-education facility reveals a variety of different positions, as does table 5.4. A distinct advantage in exploring the field of education is that most states are experiencing or will experience teacher shortages; positions are age diverse, and teacher certification can be obtained in an accelerated period of time in locations where the need exists.

Table 5.4: Examples of Education and Educational Service Career Updates

Position	Skill and Credential Updates	Update Cost and Time	Salary Potential
Director of annual giving	Bachelor's degree; previous experience in fund-raising; volunteer experience can be included	NA	$61,000
Teacher's assistant	On-the-job training; high school diploma	NA	median $23,700
Adjunct continuing-education teacher	Subject matter expert, prepared to create and teach their own course at a college or university	NA	$500 to $650 per one-day course, or course may include several sessions
English-as-second-language teacher	Four-year college degree; certifications: TESOL—Teachers of English to Speakers of Other Languages; TEFL—Teaching English as a Foreign Language; TESL—Teaching English as a Second Language	Costs and time vary	$43,910; many international opportunities
Secondary education	Bachelor's degree; shortages in math and science; licensure; alternative licensure programs for hired teachers	Costs and times vary	$43,586–$48,690

Education Notes

Make a note of any of these careers or other education-related careers that interest you. Look at job postings online and in your local news-paper. Do your homework and set up an Information Interview.

_____

_____

_____

_____

Careers in Management, Scientific, and Technical Consulting Services

The way companies conduct business is changing. More and more companies are specializing in producing and delivering goods and services for other businesses. Businesses are continuing to outsource many of their business needs: additional staffing; accounting; human resources; and consulting including management, scientific, and technical consulting services are high on the demand list. Consulting services have always been used; however, employers will need them more as they continue the lean staffing trend to be more competitive. They will have additional needs for IT, regulations, electronic commerce, and international business consultants as employees of consultant firms, contractors, and self-employed consultants. Self-employed consultants make up 27 percent of consultants.

In table 5.5, you can see that business-to-business consulting services provide an excellent opportunity to use your learned expertise in a consulting firm, in contract work, or as a self-employed consultant.

Table 5.5: Examples of Management, Scientific, and Business-to-Business Consulting (Analysts) Career Updates

Position	Skill and Credential Updates	Update Cost and Time	Salary Potential
Management, scientific, or technical consultant with consulting firm, as a contractor, or self-employed	Must have five or more years of successful expertise in area of consulting; Bachelor's with graduate degree is preferred; Consulting Management Certification is a plus; specialized certifications are often available in individual area of scientific and technical expertise	Cost and time vary	Median for management consulting: $138,000 Median for scientific consulting: $96,000 Median for technical consulting: $85,000

**Management, Scientific, and Technical
Consulting Careers Notes**

Make a note of any of these careers or other business-to-business
services careers that interest you. Do your homework. Plan an information interview with someone in the business.

_____

_____

_____

_____

Transferring corporate business skills into a career in consulting
requires unique action on your part. Keep in mind these points:

- Before you design your resume and CV, obtain several consultant position descriptions in your area of expertise. Use
  the correct and specific terminology. Highlight your related
  achievements and transferable experience.

- Consider a certification to enhance your credentials.

- Learn current trends in your business of interest through news
  reports and Internet research.

- If you are self-employed, make sure that you are good at marketing yourself, or hire someone to do this for you.

Quick-Start, No-Degree Careers

If you feel financial, mental, or emotional pressure to just get back out there soon, these careers may be just what you are looking for. The books *300 Best Jobs Without a Four-Year Degree* by Michael Farr and Laurence Shatkin (published by JIST Publishing) and *150 Jobs You Can Start Today* by Deborah Jacobson (published by Broadway Books) recommend the following quick-start careers:

Bartender and waiter

CAN (Certified Nursing Assistant)

Building inspector

Personal assistant

CPR instructor

Custom closet salesperson

Graphic designer

Home care provider

Janitorial supervisor

Landscape manager

Lawn service worker

Massage therapist

Outdoor wilderness/ teamwork instructor

Personal trainer

Pest-control provider

Security guard

School bus driver

These careers can be full time if they interest you, or they may be "survival careers" while you are developing or transitioning into a next career. Let's take a look at the credentials, costs and time involved, and annual income of a few of these careers (see table 5.6).

Table 5.6: Credential Updates for Quick-Start Practical and Unusual Positions

Position	Skill and Credential Updates	Update Cost and Time	Salary Potential
Bartender	Master Bartender designation	Two weeks; $549	$43,000
Personal Assistant	Previous administrative, travel, and event-planning experience	NA	$43,000
Wilderness team instructor and first-aid instructor	CPR, Wilderness First Responder plus wilderness experience	NA	$110–195 per day; work is often seasonal

> ### Quick-Start Practical and Unusual Career Notes
>
> Make a note of any of these quick-start practical and unusual careers that interest you and continue to look for more.
>
> _____
>
> _____
>
> _____
>
> _____

Making a Choice

One of the best things about developing a next career is that you can really "do what you've always wanted to do." You can choose permanent employment or entrepreneurial ventures including contract work, semi-permanent employment, and self-employment.

As you look at the number of diverse careers that are available to mature workers, you may be overwhelmed. How can you possibly make a decision? The answer is to narrow your search to two or three careers of interest and do your homework on the skills and credentials needed, including cost, time, and income potential. Having an information interview will also help you make a decision and choose the best source to obtain your credentials.

Take this time to carefully consider your options and choose a career that suits your interests and abilities, and is marketable in today's economy. Make sure that the earnings potential and lifestyle support your needs. And enjoy the advantage that your work experience and life wisdom bring to your career search. Look for age-diverse career opportunities where you can easily update your skills and credentials inexpensively.

Career Notes

In the spaces on the following page, create a list of all careers that interest you. Then use these Web methods of investigating the experience and credential requirements and income potential:

- Look at the *Occupational Outlook Handbook* (www.bls.gov/oco) to research positions, experience, and credentials required as well as outlook for positions of interest.

- For the most reliable salary information, check out Salary.com or Indeed, or use your search engine and type in "salary for [job title]."

- Schedule an information interview with someone in your position of interest.

Position	Skill and Credential Updates	Update Cost and Time	Salary Potential

CHAPTER 6

Designing Your *Wow!* Resume

Your goal in creating a resume is to emphasize your strengths, experience, and benefits to the hiring manager while deemphasizing too little or too much experience as well as obvious red flags such as gaps in employment. You want the hiring manager to say, "Wow! What an impressive resume. This candidate looks like a great fit for our sales management position. Her experience, strengths, and accomplishments seem to be just what we need to dramatically increase our sales and improve our key account relationships. I love how she describes herself as a flexible, change-oriented individual. I'm going to give her a call today and set up a telephone interview."

You can expect these positive results from a hiring manager, human resource professional, or recruiter when you emphasize your strengths, experience, and benefits to the buyer and deemphasize too much or too little experience and gaps in employment. But first you need to catch their attention. In this chapter you will learn to catch the reader's attention and keep it throughout the resume. And you will also learn to avoid resume pitfalls.

Catching Positive Attention with Your Resume

Your resume is your sales brochure and should be written with the objective of landing an interview. To achieve this response, you need to create an outstanding description of what you have to offer. But unfortunately, many resumes fail to survive the interviewer's quick review, which career professionals call the "30-second skim," and end up in the trash. Resumes from workers entering their second or next career are particularly vulnerable because they

- Frequently show too much experience
- Fail to show the relevance of past experiences to a new career choice
- Use antiquated career position titles
- Fail to emphasize the strengths today's employers value
- Fail to use the keywords employers are seeking in the position to be filled, and perhaps use outdated terminology
- Show obvious gaps in full-time and short-term employment

Following are some examples of resumes that failed to catch positive attention, and instead did just the opposite.

The "Too Much Experience" Ambush

Over-50 consultant to spouse: "I just don't agree with my career counselor about including only 10 to 15 years of relevant experience on my resume. I'm proud of my 35 years of experience, and darn it, I'm going to include it all!"

Negative pitfall: Workers with too many years of experience can be seen as cultural misfits, stubborn in their ways—like this consultant—and often too expensive.

This consultant's resume didn't survive the 30-second skim. Notice the hiring manager's reaction.

"Look at this summary of experience. This consultant has 35 years of experience. He must be real expensive, and given his age, I don't think he'd fit into this high-stress, high-travel environment. His objective says that he is looking for a consulting position directing human resources projects. Doesn't he know that we call what we do 'human capital management of strategic initiatives?' And why would he list 35 years of experience when we asked for only 10 to 15 years?"

The "Too Little Relevant Experience and Failure to Use Keywords" Ambush

Administrative assistant to career consultant: "I am applying for everything I think I would enjoy and am half-way qualified for. I think my background as an administrative assistant qualifies me for many positions, including medical billing. I have answered 100 ads this month on the Internet with no positive results. I'm doing my part; I think it's the economy, don't you?"

Negative pitfall: Failing to show in your resume how your experience is a transferable match to the new position. If a job posting indicates that certain training or experience is required, it normally is, unless you have a special referral into the company and they are willing to train you on the job.

Hiring manager to a colleague: "I used to get tired of looking at resumes that bear no relationship to our job requirements, but our electronic scanner weeds them out for me when they don't have the right keywords. In this case I have asked for at least two years of medical billing experience in a physician's office."

I know that you do not want to make the same mistakes as our consultant and administrative assistant. So read on to find out how to make your resume survive the 30-second skim.

Creating a Resume with Impact

When you look at a resume for the first time, what do you notice within the first 30 seconds? You probably react to the visual impact of the document (the paper color and quality, typestyle, layout, typos, punctuation, and spelling errors). Next you notice the heading (the name and contact information), the objective (the position applied for), and the qualifications summary (the professional work experience). These four areas must initially survive a hiring manager's 30-second skim and set the tone for a *Wow!* resume that will be read in its entirety and lead to an interview. Here's how to make your resume survive the 30-second skim.

In my corporate career and in my self-employment status as a career counselor, I have participated in the design of many personal advertising pieces: resumes, cover letters, brochures, and so on. Before I learned to design and produce my own brochures, a graphic artist taught me the importance of eye appeal, which she called eye candy. To achieve eye appeal, she suggested using high-quality paper; high-impact, condensed statements; easy-to-read type; bullets; and plenty of white space (space without type).

A *Wow!* resume shares many of the characteristics of good advertising copy, with two exceptions: Bold colors, and photos and designs, are not generally effective on a resume, unless you aspire to a job as an artist, actor, or advertising professional. Achieving positive visual impact with your resume involves all of the following:

- Printing on high-quality classic linen or classic laid paper in subtle colors of white, off-white, buff, or gray
- Printing in 11- or 12-point Times New Roman, Arial, or Helvetica for the body; 12-point bold for the headings (and usually all caps); and 14-point bold, usually all-caps, for your name
- Using short, high-impact statements
- Using plenty of white space and conservative bullets
- Keeping the length of the resume to one or two pages, the exception being a senior-level executive, in which case three pages is sometimes appropriate
- Keeping the text free of typos, misspelled words, and punctuation errors

Use a Bold Yet Appealing Resume Heading

Never underestimate the visual impact of your name at the top of your resume. Most of us have three or more names, sometimes hyphenated. But, similar to including all of your work experience on a resume, including all of your names or initials on a resume is not always wise. This practice confuses a hiring manager or recruiter and can create negative feelings and prejudice. For example, there are several ways you can list your name on your resume:

- **Charlene Gail Gilson Geary:** This is my full name, including my maiden name. The hiring manager/recruiter might wonder which name to call me and may see me as somewhat pretentious.

- **C. Gail Geary:** The hiring manager/recruiter might see me as being either sophisticated (positive) or pretentious (negative).

- **Gail Geary:** This name choice makes it clear that I am called Gail and it has no negative connotations. Something clear and simple like this is usually the best choice.

- **Gail Gilson-Geary:** This name shows an independent, feminist streak and an interest in highlighting a name used successfully, perhaps in business, before marriage. This name choice is also positive.

Shortly after 9/11, a client confided to me that he used M.T. Smith instead of Mohammed Smith on his resume because of ethnic prejudice (at that time). This decision worked effectively for him.

Your resume heading should include the following:

- Your name in bold (and usually in all caps, depending on the font).

- Your contact information: your address and phone numbers where you are most available. This normally includes your cell phone and your home phone if it is dedicated to you during the interview process.

- Your own e-mail address (definitely not a shared one or one belonging to your employer). Format the address as a hyperlink if you're sending the resume by e-mail.

Tip: To convert a regular-text e-mail address to a hyperlink in Microsoft Word, highlight the address and select Insert, Hyperlink from the menu. If your address doesn't already show up in the Address box, type it there. Now when an employer views your resume on the computer, all he or she has to do to send you an e-mail is click the link.

Why is including an e-mail address so important? Steve Hines, in his book *Atlanta Jobs,* wrote this: "According to a recent article in *HR Atlanta,* 85% of resumes now are sent over the Internet. Only 5% are mailed and 10% are faxed. Thus, be certain your e-mail address is formatted to hyperlink. This allows the reader to contact you immediately after reading your resume online."

Include a Clear Objective

Have you heard the expression, "Jack of all trades and master of none?" This means that someone has a little bit of knowledge in a lot of areas but has expertise in none. If your career objective is unclear, those reviewing your resume will not see how you fit the advertised (or unadvertised) position.

It is always worthwhile to create a career objective for your resume. As you read on, you can decide whether it is appropriate to include it separately or as part of your qualifications summary. I recommend using a career objective approximately 75 percent of the time.

Your career or job objective follows your heading and consists of four elements:

- The specific name or type of position you are seeking. Occasionally two position names are acceptable, such as receptionist/administrative assistant.

- The industry to which you are applying. This is preferred, but may not be possible if your resume has been designed for use in multiple industries.

- A condensed version of your strengths and skills (three is a good number) is optional and can be included in your qualifications summary.

- A statement of how you will benefit the company. This is also optional and can be included in your qualifications summary.

Write a Concise and Powerful Qualifications Summary

After you've attracted the reviewer with your heading and your objective that closely matches their job opening, what's next? Next is a powerful and concise qualifications summary of your relevant work experience for this open or soon-to-be-open position.

Your qualifications summary follows the objective and includes the following:

- A summary or condensed version of your relevant work experience included in your resume, usually going back no more than 15 years

- A description of the areas in which you excel

- Your strengths and personal characteristics

From "No Way" to "Wow! What Impact!"

To understand how the visual impact of the document, the heading, the objective, and the qualifications summary work together to create a *Wow!* resume, take a look at two entirely different examples: Maria, applying for a position as an administrative assistant, and Richard, applying for a position as a senior human capital consultant. I'll show you Before and After versions of their resumes and also suggest alternatives that can apply to your individual situation.

Before I begin working on a client's resume, I ask for a copy of their old resume and then I ask for five or six examples of open positions. You can find these on the Internet at places such as Simply Hired (www.simplyhired.com) or Indeed (www.indeed.com). In the case of some executive resumes, you can use ExecuNet (www.execunet.com) to locate by name position descriptions for which you wish to apply. The key job requirements of these open positions must be a close match to your qualifications.

Maria's Resume Gets a Makeover

MARIA SANCHEZ
220 Sunny Trace H: (708) 798-1220
San Jose, California 30987
mfoxylady@yahoo.com

Objective
An administrative assistant position in a financially secure company where I can utilitize my skills in typinging, fileing and telephone assistence.

Qualifications Summary
Over 27 years of administrative experiance with the same companyy. Excellent at tyying, fileing, handling all correspondance, and managing phone requests. Strong work ethic, never sick. Very nice, getting along with most of the staff.

Figure 6.1: Maria's Before contact info, objective, and summary.

MARIA SANCHEZ
220 Sunny Trace
San Jose, California 30907

(708) 798-1220   msanchez@yahoo.com

OBJECTIVE

An administrative assistant position emphasizing organization, attention to detail, and strong interpersonal skills to enhance office efficiency and improve internal and external customer relationships.

QUALIFICATIONS SUMMARY

Comprehensive administrative experience supporting key executives. Strong interpersonal skills including excellent written and verbal communication. People oriented, flexible team player, capable of coordinating complex projects. Adaptable, change-oriented, "can-do" individual.

Figure 6.2: Maria's After contact info, objective, and summary.

The differences between the beginnings of Maria's Before and After resumes are dramatic. The After version does the following right:

- Consistently uses an easy-to-read business font, (Times New Roman, Helvetica, or Arial are good choices) and is spell-checked

- Uses an e-mail address that is professional instead of cute

- Clearly expresses professional strengths in keywords that an interviewer would find essential for the position and that are listed in similar posted position descriptions

- Uses up-to-date business terminology in current position descriptions, replacing *typing and filing* with *enhancing office efficiency,* and so on

- Shows how the company will benefit from Maria instead of how Maria will benefit from it

Maria replaced the verb *utilizing* with *emphasizing,* which has a more professional ring. In the After version of her qualifications summary, Maria did the following:

- Created an ageless resume by referring to comprehensive experience instead of listing her years.

- Upgraded her business vocabulary to sound more current and at a professionally higher level, such as *people oriented* and *coordinating complex projects.*

- Mentioned strengths that are valued in today's business community, for example, *adaptable, change-oriented* instead of *reliable, never sick.* These qualities are important, but the wording is antiquated and the qualities are expected.

- Used energetic language: *flexible, capable of coordinating complex projects,* and *"can-do" individual.*

- Eliminated all spelling errors.

Variations on the Objective and Qualifications Summary

- For two or more definitely related positions, separate the position titles with a forward slash, as in Customer Service/Inside Sales.

- If the name of the position is not clear, use a general description such as "a position in healthcare management."

- In a high-level executive position such as Senior Vice President of Communications, combine the objective into the qualifications summary, as shown in Richard's resume (see figure 6.4).

- Depending on the position you are seeking, you can also refer to the Qualifications Summary as the Executive Summary or Summary of Experience.

- Using bullets in a qualifications summary is optional, but can add to clarity and visual impact.

- If your address may be perceived by an employer as an extremely long commute, consider omitting the address from the resume and listing a local phone number. If asked your address, be honest and indicate that you have no problem with a long commute.

Richard's Resume Moves into Wow!ness

Richard's Before resume needed help to survive the 30-second skim. It lacked executive presence and currency, and emphasized his age. Let's see what he did to make it pop out.

RICHARD SMITHSON
rsmithson@att.net
587 Mulberry Street   H: 678-222-9433
Cincinnati, Ohio 33957   cell: 678-503-9954

Objective

A position as a Senior Human Resources Consultant.

Executive Summary

35 successful years of directing human resources projects. Strengths include exemplary leadership and excellent interpersonal skills. Reliable, dependable, and client oriented.

Figure 6.3: Richard's Before contact info, objective, and summary.

Richard Smithson

rsmithson@att.net

587 Mulberry Street   Home: 678-222-9433
Cincinnati, Ohio 33957   Mobile: 678-503-9954

Executive Summary

Senior Human Capital Consultant with extensive experience in directing technology software initiatives in insurance, healthcare, and biotech industries. Strengths in team leadership, technology application, and client development will contribute to dramatic income growth and client satisfaction. Recognized for

- Innovative HR technology applications
- Team leadership
- Project management
- Client business development
- Staff training and development
- Critical problem solving

Figure 6.4: Richard's After contact info, objective, and summary.

Richard and I elected to combine his objective and qualifications into a strong executive summary, often considered more appropriate for key executive positions. His improved executive summary does the following:

- Uses the latest position terminology and keywords.

- Uses the term *extensive experience,* which is ageless, rather than the phrase *35 years of experience.*

- Is specific in industries serviced.

- Highlights specific consulting expertise in the paragraph and the bullets.

- Tells what Richard offers the employer.

- Employs a larger-sized (12-point text and heading and 14-point name) and a uniform and appropriate font (Arial) for a more attractive visual impact. Up to two fonts are okay.

- Uses an e-mail hyperlink for the Internet version.

Be sure to view the position description if posted to see the years of experience the job requires, but keep in mind that employers are generally looking for no more than 10 to 15 years of relevant work experience. Including more years of experience in your objective or qualifications summary may cause a hiring manager to conclude that you may be lacking in energy and may not fit in culturally. Also, too experienced often translates to too expensive in an employer's eyes. Why create a red flag in your objective or summary? You can make your resume ageless by reducing the number of years indicated in your summary or using the terms *comprehensive, extensive,* and *diverse.*

Getting Your Resume Makeover

How can you improve on your objective and qualifications summary? Don't think that you can quickly complete these tasks. It takes several hours to write a really good objective and summary. Never take the one-size-fits-all approach by sending out a resume with an objective or summary that doesn't match the position for which you are applying. Remain flexible.

Find comparable job descriptions on the Internet, and then alter your objective and summary to closely match an actual posted position description. Include the keywords found in the job description, company newsletter, or articles. When you are finished, read over your work to make sure that your summary is consistent with your objective.

What Will You Say in Your Objective and Summary?

Write your career objective in the space provided. Include the specific name of the position, the industry, your strengths, and how you as an employee will help the employer. Writing the objective even when you intend to use just a qualifications or executive summary will help you focus on what you really want. Write your objective first and then your qualifications summary.

Objective

_____

_____

_____

Qualifications Summary

_____

_____

_____

An objective and summary that pass the 30-second skim, are ageless, and create a *Wow!* impression are always the result of hard work. Powerful resumes pay off in spades but not only in interviews; they also create the potential for a higher salary offer.

Designing Stand-Out Achievements and Accomplishments

Potential employers look closely at achievements and accomplishments. In fact, many share with me that this is their number-one measurement of candidates on paper. In my opinion, the most challenging part of composing a resume is transforming your duties and responsibilities into achievements and accomplishments. But when you do this, the payoff is tremendous. You will have a standout *Wow!* resume.

When I left corporate America 16 years ago to start my own business, I had not written a resume in 16 years. I read a number of resume books and sought professional help in composing my resume. When I showed it to a college friend, she said, "Who is this woman? I had no idea how much you have accomplished." My self-esteem went up 10 notches!

Asking Questions About Your Achievements

As Maria and Richard began writing their achievements and accomplishments, I asked them to answer the questions in the following worksheet to jog their memories about their accomplishments. Take a few minutes to answer them, too.

A Checklist to Discover Your Accomplishments (Include Past Career and Volunteer Experience)

Have you...

❏ Saved the company money? How? How much?

_____

_____

❏ Increased sales? How? How much?

_____

_____

❏ Designed, created, or developed something original or for the first time? What? What is the benefit of it?

_____

_____

❏ Received an award or recognition? Why? For what?

_____

_____

❏ Been promoted or upgraded? Why?

_____

_____

❏ Accomplished more with fewer resources or increased efficiency? How?

_____

_____

(continued)

(continued)

❏ Increased production or reduced downtime? How? How much?

_____

❏ Managed, supervised, or trained a department or team? How many? With what results?

_____

_____

❏ Managed a budget? How much? Successful results?

_____

_____

❏ Identified and solved a difficult problem or problems involving people, systems, or equipment? What? With what results?

_____

_____

❏ Established a new record in safety, sales, or customer service? What? Explain with specifics.

_____

_____

Hopefully that was a feel-good activity for you that made you see how much you have accomplished in your past jobs or in volunteer activities. Carefully composing your accomplishments will raise your self-esteem.

The Right Wording

When you work with a list of questions like those in the preceding worksheet, you have an excellent starting point for writing bulleted accomplishments. As you will see in examples that follow, these accomplishments are listed under each employer in a chronological resume and are grouped together under a Selected Accomplishments heading in a functional resume. As you write, keep in mind these suggestions:

- Write a condensed version of your accomplishment, as a bulleted item; a sentence or two is enough.

- Begin each accomplishment with a strong action verb such as designed, led, saved, and so on, but be careful to vary the action verbs so that your reader doesn't lose interest.

- Start with the result first, as in this example: "Reduced customers' complaints by 75% in 90-day period; promoted to Customer Service Supervisor."

- Although you should avoid personal pronouns, such as *I* or *we,* write the accomplishment in such a way as to claim personal responsibility for the achievement while acknowledging that others contributed to your success. For example, "Achieved new business goal of $2.5M in 2008."

- Use specific numbers, achievement dates, and company names to add reality and credibility. (Reasonable estimations that you can explain are acceptable.)

- Make sure that each accomplishment you list will not achieve a "so what?" response.

- Consider each accomplishment a mini-story that uses the STAR approach. What was the Situation? What was your Task? What Action did you take? What was the positive Result?

The Best Organization

When it comes to writing a resume, identifying your accomplishments is only half the battle; organizing them is the other half. If you completed the preceding achievements worksheet and then listed them on your resume just as they appeared in the worksheet, you probably would have an organizational mess. How can you untangle them all and present them clearly? I have three words for you: functional, chronological, and hybrid. All three are methods of organizing resumes.

The Functional Resume Format

A functional resume format is appropriate in any of these situations:

- You have a broken work history or are changing occupations.

- You have an unsteady career progression.

- You don't want to highlight your latest employer.

- You want to minimize your years of experience.

■ You have worked for the same employer for many years and want to emphasize selected functions within your positions.

With a functional resume you can either group all bulleted accomplishments under Selected Accomplishments, or you can list the accomplishments under functional headings such as Team Leadership, Instructional Design, and Delivery Training. These headings can show how you qualify for the requirements of a new position based on your past experience.

In using a functional resume, follow these tips:

■ When you use functional headings to group accomplishments (effective, but not mandatory), use up to five accomplishments per heading.

■ Use up to 10 accomplishments if you are not separating these by functional headings.

■ Do not worry about putting the accomplishments and responsibilities in chronological order.

■ List your employment information in chronological order in a professional experience section later in the resume.

The functional resume format offers many benefits for a mature worker. It highlights accomplishments and deemphasizes age. If you are changing careers, you can select the accomplishments that point toward your new position. If you are having a hard time identifying accomplishments and responsibilities, you can create five or six instead of having to place three under each employer when you have multiple employers. Using the functional format is also a good idea if you are including volunteer experience in your resume or you have gaps in your employment. In Maria's case, a one-page resume, we eliminated earlier employment situations so as not to date her and used a functional resume format.

The Chronological Resume Format

A chronological format lists jobs in the order that they occurred and keeps accomplishments under each job title. This format is appropriate when you have unbroken work history, you are continuing in the same occupation, and you have progressive responsibilities. Your latest employer is highlighted because it is listed first.

The Hybrid Resume Format

There is one other type of resume, the hybrid, which is a combination of functional and chronological elements. To create one, you first design a functional resume and then separately add one or two professional accomplishments under each employer listed. I have not used this resume with my clients because I list the employer's name or circumstance in the functional accomplishments, which clearly belong to an employer. But the benefit of the hybrid resume is that the hiring manager can see even more clearly which accomplishment belongs to each employer.

Because this resume type heavily derives from the two main resume types, I do not include a sample of it in this chapter.

From "So What?" to "Wow! What Accomplishments!"

It's fun to brainstorm and write as many accomplishments as you can think of for each position you've held. Now, let's make it easy on the HR professional or recruiter who is reviewing your resume. Follow these tips:

- Include achievements/accomplishments that are most relevant to the position you're applying for.
- Use at least two and generally no more than seven achievements per position.
- Arrange them with the most significant as the first and last under each position.
- Consider boldfacing outstanding savings, sales figures, and so on, but don't overdo it.
- Keep each bullet to one or two lines if possible.

Maria's Functional Resume

Let's take a look at two versions of Maria Sanchez's accomplishments, before and after, along with her education and skills.

SELECTED ACCOMPLISHMENTS

- I participated as part of a team to plan luncheons, retirements, and appreciation dinners.
- Entered office expenses, purchased supplies, and renewed all vehicle titles, license registrations, and service records.
- Saved 25% by changing kitchen supplier.

EDUCATION

Graduated-Roosevelt High School, San Francisco, CA.

Figure 6.5: Maria's functional accomplishments, Before.

Now here are the changes we made to these sections of Maria's resume. We also added a few more accomplishments in the final version.

SELECTED ACCOMPLISHMENTS

- Recognized by President of Value Mart (VM) for effective coordination of luncheons, retirements, and appreciation dinners.
- Handled all details of office budgeting, invoicing, purchasing of supplies, and fleet record maintenance at VM.
- Saved 25% ($5,000 annually) by changing kitchen supplier for Maritime Oil.

EDUCATION

Graduated–Roosevelt High School, San Francisco, CA

PROFESSIONAL TRAINING

- Time Management (2004)
- Excel and PowerPoint (2003)

SKILLS

Microsoft Office, Excel, PowerPoint, QuickBooks Pro Accounting Software

MEMBERSHIPS

Toastmasters International; President, San Jose Chapter of American Business Women's Association

---

Figure 6.6: Maria's functional accomplishments, After.

You can see how Maria improved on her accomplishments by giving herself full credit; removing personal pronouns; using stronger, more professional language; and providing specific dollar numbers. If you can't think of enough accomplishments (3 to 10), you can change the heading to Selected Accomplishments and Responsibilities and add significant responsibilities. If you worked as a team and do not feel comfortable claiming full credit, use these phrases:

- Played a key role in
- Collaborated with
- Instrumental in

There was no reason to rewrite Maria's education section. She did not include dates of high school and college graduations, and neither should you unless they are within 10 years. If you did not graduate or receive a degree, use phrases like *Attended, Studies in,* or *course hours* and then list the degree program of the majority of your courses. Include professional training, along with recent dates of completion, showing a positive interest in continuing education.

I recommended that Maria include her skills as an administrative assistant at the end of her resume. However, administrative assistant, IT, telecommunications, and software engineering positions are considered technical and require technical resumes. Skills for these positions can be effectively included after the qualifications summary. For many other industries and position types, skills are not included in a separate section.

I encouraged Maria to add memberships to her resume because they show relevance to her career objective in terms of communication and leadership. Do not include memberships, affiliations, or associations that have no relevance to your career position or are controversial or religiously affiliated, such as Member of Brittany Spaniel Club, Weight Watchers International, and Emanuel Evangelical Church. If your interviewer hates dogs, is a skinny Minnie, or is of another faith, these memberships could work against you.

Generally, I would not include a section on personal interests unless they are directly related to the position you're applying for or show exceptional mental or physical energy for your age, for example, current International Chess Champion or Completed New York Marathon, 2008.

Maria's final resume was this one-page *Wow!* beauty:

MARIA SANCHEZ
220 Sunny Trace
San Jose, California 30987

(708) 798-1220   msanchez@yahoo.com

OBJECTIVE

An administrative assistant position emphasizing organization, attention to detail, and strong interpersonal skills to enhance office efficiency and improve internal and external customer relationships.

QUALIFICATIONS SUMMARY

Comprehensive administrative experience supporting key executives. Strong interpersonal skills including excellent written and verbal communication. People oriented, flexible team player, capable of coordinating complex projects. Adaptable, change-oriented, "can-do" individual.

SELECTED ACCOMPLISHMENTS

- Recognized by President of Value Mart (VM) for effective coordination of luncheons, retirements, and appreciation dinners.
- Handled all details of office budgeting, invoicing, purchasing of supplies, and fleet record maintenance at VM.
- Saved 25% ($5,000 annually) by changing kitchen supplier for Maritime Oil.

PROFESSIONAL EXPERIENCE

Value Mart, San Jose, CA   1994–2009
Senior Executive Administrative Assistant
Administrative Assistant/Distribution

Maritime Oil, Houston, TX
Executive Secretary   1990–1994

EDUCATION

Graduated–Roosevelt High School, San Francisco, CA

PROFESSIONAL TRAINING

- Time Management (2004)
- Excel and PowerPoint (2003)

SKILLS

Microsoft Office, Excel, PowerPoint, QuickBooks Pro Accounting Software

MEMBERSHIPS

Toastmasters International; President, San Jose Chapter of America n Business Women's Association

Figure 6.7: Maria's final resume.

Richard's Chronological Resume

Now take a look at Richard's achievements as part of his chronological resume. Richard and I selected a chronological resume because of his consistent pattern of work history, and because we could easily drop off an earlier employer. In a chronological resume, accomplishments are listed after each employer under the Professional Experience heading.

Professional Experience

Anderson Consulting, Washington, D.C. 1998-2009
Senior Consultant
Responsible for PeopleSoft applications over a two-year period. Client was happy that we came in on time and under budget.
Trained and managed all consultants in the Northeast Region.

Education

BS Business, University of Maryland
MBA George Washington University

Professional Certifications
FSA; People Soft Certification: PMI Certification

Figure 6.8: Richard's Before accomplishments.

Now here are the changes we made to these sections of Richard's resume.

Professional Experience

Anderson Consulting, Washington, D.C.   1998–2009
Senior Consultant

- Formally acknowledged by Capitol Insurance Group and by Anderson for leading effective custom installation of PeopleSoft program nationwide.

- Recognized as key player in $10 million income growth for NE region in 2007 because of effective training and management of 60 consultants and associates.

Education

BS, Business, University of Maryland
MBA, George Washington University

Professional Certifications
FSA; PeopleSoft Certification: PMI Certification

Professional Affiliations

DC Insurance Institute; outgoing president, SHRM (Society for Human Resource Management)

Figure 6.9: Richard's After accomplishments and extras.

The change we made to the first achievement involved adding specifics: the name of the software, the client, and the project scope. We used a strong action verb, *acknowledged,* preceded by a strong adverb, *formally.* Additionally, the mention of an HR technology application and team leadership is consistent with the executive summary. We agreed that additional professional experience should follow with two to seven accomplishments under each employer.

For Richard, the professional certifications and affiliations areas enhance his resume because of their career relevance.

Following is Richard's *Wow!* consulting resume. This resume, like Rome, was certainly not built in one day. It was crafted with professional help and represents about 12 hours of work together. A resume will continue to be a work in progress for you. The results of a well-crafted resume are worth the effort, however.

Richard Smithson

rsmithson@att.net

587 Mulberry Street   Home: 678-222-9433
Cincinnati, Ohio 33957   Mobile: 678-503-9954

Executive Summary

Senior Human Capital Consultant with extensive experience in directing
technology software initiatives in insurance, healthcare, and biotech industries.
Strengths in team leadership, technology application, and client development will
contribute to dramatic income growth and client satisfaction. Recognized for

- Innovative HR technology applications
- Team leadership
- Project management
- Client business development
- Staff training and development
- Critical problem solving

Professional Experience

Anderson Consulting, Washington, D.C.   1998–2009
Senior Consultant

- Formally acknowledged by Capitol Insurance Group and by Anderson for
  leading effective custom installation of PeopleSoft program nationwide.

- Recognized as key player in $10 million income growth for NE region in 2007
  because of effective training and management of 60 consultants and
  associates.

Education

BS, Business, University of Maryland
MBA, George Washington University

Professional Certifications

FSA; PeopleSoft Certification: PMI Certification

Professional Affiliations

DC Insurance Institute; outgoing president, SHRM (Society for Human Resource
Management)

Figure 6.10: Richard's final resume.

Review: Features of the Three Resume Types

Let's review the features of the two types of resumes developed in this chapter: Maria's functional resume and Richard's chronological one. Remember that you can use skills, professional certifications, and affiliations on either resume.

I have included the characteristics of all three resume types below.

Table 6.1: Characteristics of Resume Types

Functional Resume	Chronological Resume	Hybrid Resume
Name, address, phone, e-mail	Name, address, phone, e-mail	Name, address, phone, e-mail
Objective (in most cases)	Objective (in most cases)	Objective (in most cases)
Qualifications Summary	Qualifications Summary	Qualifications Summary
Selected accomplishments (can be put under a functional area of expertise if desired)		Selected Accomplishments (can be put under a functional area of expertise if desired)
Professional Experience	Professional Experience (including selected accomplishments under each employer)	Professional Experience with a couple of accomplishments under each employer
Education/Professional Training	Education/Professional Training	Education/Professional Training
Military Service (optional)	Military Service (optional)	Military Service (optional)

Writing and Polishing Your Accomplishments

Now it's time for you to write your own accomplishments.

Vary Your Action Verbs

To make your resume interesting, vary the action verbs you use to begin each accomplishment. If you find yourself using the same verbs, highlight the overused verb and look under Tools, Language, Thesaurus in Microsoft Word and choose a synonym to replace it. If you prefer, you can use a hard-copy dictionary or thesaurus for the same purpose. Table 6.2 gives a short list of action verbs for you to use.

Table 6.2: Examples of Action Verbs

achieved	controlled	engineered	improved	motivated
approved	corrected	exceeded	increased	negotiated
arranged	created	forecasted	initiated	organized
assembled	decreased	generated	invented	procured
budgeted	directed	hired	led	received
conducted	edited	identified	managed	recognized

Use the STAR Method to Write Your Accomplishments

The STAR approach is a method of telling a story of an accomplishment involving the following elements:

- S (situation)
- T (task)
- A (the action you took)
- R (the positive results)

Maria used this method in writing her achievements. For example, she wrote this: "Saved 25% ($5,000 annually) by changing kitchen supplier." Maria put the results first, followed by the action she took. The Situation and Task were understood in her statement, but they also can be expressed in more detail.

Accomplishments Key Points

Remember these key points in writing your accomplishments:

- Use strong, varied action verbs.

- Avoid pronouns.

- Put the results first, if possible.

- Give details and specifics, such as numbers and percents.

- Give each accomplishment this "so what?" test: Will the accomplishment Wow! the interviewer?

- Accept responsibility for your major contributions.

- Occasionally intersperse important responsibilities that do not seem to be full accomplishments. Example: Managed high volume of travel/meeting arrangements for Senior Vice President of Sales, Regional Sales Manager, and National Account Executive.

What Accomplishments Will You Include on Your Resume?

Write three of your accomplishments. Leave the unnumbered lines empty for now.

I. _____

_____

_____

_____

_____

_____

_____

2. _____

_____

_____

_____

_____

3. _____

_____

_____

_____

_____

_____

Go back and confirm that each accomplishment follows the guidelines recommended earlier in this chapter. If it does not, revise it to make it *Wow!* your resume audience.

Add your professional experience, education, professional training, military experience, skills, professional credentials, and professional memberships/affililiations if applicable.

Professional Experience

_____

_____

_____

Education

_____

_____

_____

Professional Training

_____

_____

_____

Military Experience

_____

_____

(continued)

109

(continued)

Skills

_____

_____

_____

Professional Credentials

_____

_____

_____

Professional Memberships/Affiliations

_____

_____

_____

Summing Up

Now you have created the important elements of a *Wow!* resume in a functional, chronological, or hybrid format.

When you have completed your resume, ask yourself these questions:

- ❏ Does my resume create a strong, positive visual impact: enough white space, quality paper stock, appropriate font size and typestyle, appropriate use of bullets? And, of course, no typos, spelling, or punctuation errors?

- ❏ Have I chosen the best format (chronological, functional, or hybrid) to present my strengths?

- ❏ Have I stated a clear objective that matches the employer's position description, separately or in the summary?

- ❏ Have I created a dynamic summary of experience highlighting my experience and strengths?

- ❏ Will my resume survive the 30-second skim?

- ❏ Does my resume highlight my accomplishments and deemphasize my age?

❏ Are my accomplishments dynamic, and do they support my objective?

❏ Will my resume cause the interviewer to say *"Wow!"*?

Don't forget that many resources are available to help you write a resume, but you are the heart of it. A resume consultant or free software program such as Microsoft Office templates can provide you with an attractive format, but you must supply the dynamic information. You can find these free templates by going to http:// office.microsoft.com and looking under the Templates tab. The only problem with using a template is that your resume style can be limited; for example, many templates have a wide left margin, which limits your use of space. I personally do not use templates for this reason. Also, most other offers of templates are a come-on for a resume writer's business.

Career consultants and well-written resume guides—such as *Résumé Magic* by Susan Britton Whitcomb and *Gallery of Best Resumes* by David Noble (both published by JIST Publishing), as well as *Resume Power* by Tom Washington (published by Mount Vernon Press)— can guide you in appropriate language and phraseology. And don't forget that there are specialized resume books for technical, sales, healthcare, and numerous other types of career positions.

Getting Your Resume into the Hands of a Hiring Professional

Now that you have a *Wow!* resume, what is the best way to get your resume into the hands of a hiring professional? Absolutely the best way to deliver your resume is to have a networking contact or executive recruiter hand-deliver it or e-mail it to the hiring professional with his or her recommendation. Delivering your resume this way ensures that it will not get lost in the pile of 1,000 resumes that are sent in through a heavily used Web site such as Monster.com.

The next best practice is to send your resume by standard mail to the hiring manager with a dynamic cover letter, unless company instructions require that your resume be sent in a text-only version through the company's Web site. In this case, follow the instructions, but also have your networking contact put in a good word for you after you have submitted your resume. Because the majority of resumes are delivered electronically, yours will stand out when it is delivered with a personal touch that separates you from the crowd.

Trends in Text-Only Scannable Resumes and Portfolios

Many clients entering their second and subsequent careers do not know that they will probably need to create a separate text-only, scannable resume in addition to their regular resume. The best techniques for creating them change every few years. Do not make the mistake of simply copying and pasting your regular resume into a box on an employer's Web site or job board. Although your resume will be scannable (electronically readable), it will come out in an uneven format and it will not be maximized with an essential keyword section.

Text-Only Resumes

The text-only resume is basically a block version of your resume without any formatting, with a keyword summary on top. Following is an example of a text-only resume with a keyword summary above the text.

KEYWORDS

Executive Assistant, Administrative Assistant, Administrative Manager, Human Resources Assistant, Office Support, Operations Support, Technology Support, Interviewing, Recruiting, Interpersonal Skills, Communication, New Hire Orientation, HR Project Management, Meeting Coordination, HR Legalities, Expense and Performance Improvement, Microsoft Office, Word, Excel, PowerPoint, Web-based Research, QuickBooks, Administrative Skills, People Skills, Employee Training, HRIS System Reviews, Employee Data, Vendor Contracts, Payroll, Personnel Issues, Analytical Skills, Attention to Detail, Medicaid, Legal and Medical Terminology, Benefits Manager, Community Involvement, Emory University, BS Urban Life, Criminal Justice.

JANET ANGELICO

18120 Willow Lane

Houston, TX 30004

jangelo@gmail.com

912-444-3820

Executive Assistant / Administrative Assistant / Administrative Manager

QUALIFICATIONS SUMMARY

Accomplished business professional with in-depth experience in office support and administration of human resources, operations, and technology applications including programming and Web-based research. Intelligent, organized, and detail-oriented with excellent interpersonal skills, both written and oral.

Core competencies include:

*Interviewing
*Listening
*New Hire Orientation
*Management of HR Projects
*Coordination of Meetings, Conferences, Schedules
*Understanding of Legalities Involving Employment
*Creation and Maintenance of Databases
*Expense and Performance Improvement
*Adept in Microsoft Office, Word, Excel, PowerPoint, Web-based Research, QuickBooks

(continued)

(continued)

```
SELECTED ACCOMPLISHMENTS AND RESPONSIBILITIES

*Promoted from Administrative Support I to Administrative
Support II and Administrative Support III at Offshore Oil
because of excellent people skills, administrative skills,
and motivation.

*Provided human resources support for staff interviews and
new-hire orientation and training for Consulting, Inc.,
both locally and nationally.

EMPLOYMENT

EDUCATION

COMMUNITY INVOLVEMENT
```

Figure 6.11: Sample text-only resume (abbreviated).

For complete instructions on how to create a text-only resume, see my full list of resources and links at www.atlantacareertransition. com/resources/index/php.

Standing Out from the Crowd

Recent trends to make your *Wow!* resume stand out from the crowd are to make it a part of a portfolio, either in hard copy placed in an attractive presentation folder or as a Web page. My take on the Web page route is that this is a cool idea if you are currently employed or unemployed with financial reserves, Internet savvy, and plenty of time to be creative in your job search. If this does not fit you, don't embrace this idea. I have written the language in HTML for my Web site, and I can attest to the fact that this is very time-consuming. On the other hand, creating a hard-copy resume portfolio is not time-consuming and makes your resume stand out from the crowd.

I recently helped Sam, a CAD designer (a creator of architectural renderings for engineers and architects), create a hard-copy resume portfolio, which consisted of the following:

- A silver/gray glossy pocket portfolio purchased at an office-supply store
- His attractive personal business card

- His *Wow!* resume
- Colored samples of his design renderings

We produced a targeted mailing of 50 major architectural and engineering firms. Whenever Sam called to request an interview, he was always positively recognized. The recruiter or hiring manager never trashed his resume portfolio, and yes, he was soon employed.

You might ask yourself, "What can I include in a resume portfolio? I'm no graphic designer." Well, you can include letters of recommendation, awards, published articles, success stories created from your work experience, and any exceptional work samples.

It always pays to go the extra mile to create a *Wow!* resume, not just in terms of being called for an interview, but also in terms of the future salary you can command.

Sometimes It Pays to Be Different

There are always exceptions to the resume protocol I have covered. I have erred on the side of conservatism because I want you to stand out positively, not negatively. Having said this, I give you license to include your own individual resume touches: a different font for a "different for you" heading, a positive testimonial quotation in your accomplishments, an oversized envelope for resume mailing, and so on. Just make sure that your resume is attention getting and tasteful.

Resume Planning

Now, let's do some resume planning before you move on by answering these questions:

- What resume style will you use? Chronological, functional, or a combination of the two?

  _____

- What do you need to change to make your resume awesome?

  _____

  _____

- Should you have more than one resume so that you do not look like a "jack of all trades"?

  _____

  _____

- Do you need to be working with both a regular resume and a text-only resume?

  _____

  _____

CHAPTER 7

Designing Your *Wow!* Promotional Material

When you are looking for a job, you'll use promotional materials such as your resume, cover letter, business card, and thank-you note. All other correspondence you send out, including e-mail, is also part of your public image. These materials make a positive or negative statement about your identity. If you want to be a self-employed entrepreneur, your promotional materials will include all of the above plus a Web site, a brochure, and product packaging.

You are also a part of your promotional package, which includes how you look, speak, and act.

Never forget that your own persona—how you look, speak, and act—is often your strongest advertisement.

In chapter 6, "Designing Your *Wow!* Resume," you began to design your promotional materials. In this chapter I will go step-by-step through designing your business card, cover letter, curriculum vitae, success stories, business brochure, and Web site.

Six Elements of Great Promotional Design

When you look at an attractive business card, a one-page business description, or an e-mail, what are the features that positively stand out to you? What features turn you off? From my experience working with three talented graphic designers and two webmasters, I have created a list of six elements of promotional design that I consider the gold standard. You can remember them by the acronym, **AAAACC** (and no, I don't expect you to pronounce this):

- Appeal, visual and tactile: You can get this through an easy-to-read format with plenty of white space, appropriate fonts, use of color, and fine paper. Remember to use left-to-right placement, which is the way the eye travels.

- Attention-getting devices: Use of attention-getting devices at the beginning of printed material, such as a quotation about yourself or your business, or photographs.

- Audience involvement: Asking questions in the material and making the piece interactive with the audience.

- Appropriateness of design and consistency of all promotional material: The design is appropriate for its use and is complimentary with all other promotional material you use.

- Correct grammar, spelling, punctuation and word choice: This goes without saying.

- Clarity of material: The piece answers the important questions of *Who? What? When? Where? Why?* and *How?*

How do you know that you have achieved an awesome promotional piece? You are sincerely complimented on it; your material passes the side-by-side test when placed next to "best-of-its-kind" promotional material; and, most importantly, the piece gets results in the form of an interview or a call for information about your business or product.

The Major Types of Promotional Material

Now let's take a look at the major promotional pieces job seekers and entrepreneurs use when promoting themselves and their businesses. We'll rate them using the AAAACC acronym.

Business Cards

After the traditional resume and the text-only resume, the business card is the most important promotional piece for a job seeker or entrepreneur. Here is a business card sample for a recent client with the name and phone numbers changed. Rate it by the above acronym.

GERRY SMITH
Sales and Sales Management of
Medical Devices • Medical Disposables
Biotech • Healthcare Products

(770) 222-8888
gerrysmith@comcast.net

Figure 7.1: Sample business card (front).

Expertise
- *Sales and Sales Management*
- *Increasing Geographic Market Share*
- *National Accounts, Integrated Delivery Networks*
- *Hiring, Training, Motivating*
- *Coaching & Mentoring Sales Teams*

#1 International Sales Manager 5 years in a row!

Figure 7.2: Sample business card (back).

This job seeker's business card gets a 100 percent score in my book. It uses the back to share expertise and leaves off the home address so that his small-town location is not a deterrent. It fits the acronym AAAACC. It involves the audience by inviting them to contact Gerry at the telephone number or e-mail address listed.

Cover Letters

The idea for the cover letter in figure 7.3 is taken from the book *Selling to VITO* by Anthony Parinello. VITO does not refer to a mafia don, but stands for *Very Important Top Officer*, the hiring manager or above.

Use this type of cover letter when you are mailing a copy of your resume. Use a shortened, modified version when you're using e-mail or applying online. Put your cover letter on letterhead stationery. If you send it in an e-mail, be sure to include contact information.

Draft your own quote and seek former supervisors to endorse it, or take one from a performance review. This is the attention-getting statement.

"xxx has demonstrated the ability to supervise legislative and legal research and provide inspired direction to staff. I highly recommend her for the position of Auto Safety and Regulatory Affairs Manager." —**John Marin COO**

Date

Include exact name and/or position reference number.

Formal title of addressee
Company name and address

Re: Auto Safety and Regulatory Affairs Manager

Dear Marilyn,

Get on a first-name basis. Call and obtain the name of the hiring manager or VITO.

I am an accomplished attorney and public health professional with proven expertise in the following areas:

- Management of staff and resources to achieve organizational goals.
- Direction of research in automobile safety, fuel economy, and other related issues.
- Development and management of fund-raising and grant proposals.
- Collaboration with governmental decision makers, consumer groups, and allied organizations to achieve support for issues.

I am particularly interested in working for (name of company) because of your success in consumer advocacy. I will benefit (name of company) through my experience and record of high achievement.

I am interested in exploring how I may become a valuable resource to your organization and am enclosing my resume for your consideration. I will call you on Monday, August 5th, at 10:00 a.m. to see whether we might schedule a convenient time to meet. I thank you in advance for your consideration.

Sincerely,

Your name
Add phone and e-mail address

Figure 7.3: Sample cover letter.

What makes this letter stand out is the attention-getting headline, using a first name, selling benefits versus features, and making a sincere callback effort. How does this cover letter measure up against yours and against the acronym AAAACC? I would give it 125 percent. Some of my clients have expressed reservations about the callback time, saying, "I know that the IT Director or VP of Sales will not be there when I call him." This may or may not be true. But the letter shows a seriousness of effort on your part, which favorably impresses most hiring managers and will result in contact success if you continue in pursuit of this business.

All other correspondence, including e-mail messages, should also meet the AAAACC test and represent your best professional promotional effort. Don't forget the appearance of all envelopes and thank-you cards. They are part of your promotional identity. Keep thank-you cards as simple and professional as possible.

Promotional Materials for Products and Services

Next, let's look at promotional materials for an entrepreneur who is offering a product or service. The business card we outlined for job seekers in figures 7.1 and 7.2 applies perfectly for business uses, too. Business owners can add a tasteful logo or picture as part of the process of establishing a consistent, distinctive image (branding).

Today's entrepreneurs also need a CV, a brochure, success stories, and a Web site.

The CV

Let's start with the CV (or one-page or profile). Note that it is appropriate to include a picture or logo on the left side of the page. I prepared the following CV for one of my successful entrepreneurial clients, Larry Sanders.

LARRY SANDERS,
SANDERS & ASSOCIATES INTERNATIONAL, LLC
Exceeding Expectations Through Excellence in Execution (4E)

Larry is an accomplished senior manager with a solid track record in leading domestic and international programs. His passions include turnaround and diverse, multifunctional project management opportunities—especially succeeding with complex projects, world-class operations, and strategic planning for business growth.

Larry is a results-driven, hands-on leader with expertise in global product supply systems, manufacturing operations, and capital and initiative management execution. Larry's proven expertise in motivating technical and non-technical resources creates the ideal environment to deliver stretch objectives, improve productivity , and increase profits. Selected accomplishments include the following:

- Led global organizational initiative for major Latin American paper manufacturer, unifying R&D, engineering, and operational resources—**reducing product launch time from 12 to 6 months.**
- Directed operational initiative for new high-speed proprietary process and automated equipment platform for consumer goods manufacturer—**achieving 100% productivity gain.**
- Delivered a turn-around success for a complex product supply capability project—**launching 3 months ahead of schedule and with a 20% capital reduction.**

Larry is known for his ability to approach situations from a variety of perspectives, having worked in both hands-on and executive-level leadership roles. Executives rely on Larry for his no-nonsense approach and commitment to deliver beyond expectations. Operating managers, technicians, and project execution resources trust his commitment and thrive on his even-handed, people-focused manner.

Prior to founding Sanders & Associates International, Larry worked throughout North and South America fulfilling roles including plant engineering leader, operations manager, plant contact and site project manager, regional project manager, regional executive, and global program manager for Procter & Gamble and Exxon. He is proud of delivering benchmark results in 10 different product lines and 6 different countries.

A graduate of the Georgia Institute of Technology with a Bachelor of Science in Civil Engineering, Larry is also a Certified Expert in Project Management and Capital Management. He is a member of the Project Management Institute, Institute of Six Sigma Professionals, American Management Association, International Institute for Learning, and American Society for Training and Development. Larry is fluent in Spanish and conversational with Portuguese.

At Sanders & Associates International, we are committed to providing **affordable, experienced-based training, mentoring, consulting, and hands-on leadership** supporting your strategic project management programs and manufacturing requirements. Our focus areas and strengths include the following:

Strategy	Operations	Revenue Growth	Human Resources
• Strategy Development & Deployment • Operational Structure Development	• Project Management & Product Launch • Process & Procedure Development • Supplier / Customer Interface	• New Business Development • Business Valuation & Acquisition • Supply Chain Loss Analysis	• Technology Transfer & Training • High-Performance Work Systems • Recruitment & Retention

Contact Larry Sanders, Sanders & Associates International, LLC
678-362-4999, sandersle@comcast.net

Figure 7.4: Larry's CV.

The CV can be used by job seekers and entrepreneurs and is inexpensive to produce. It is especially suitable for applying for adjunct training and teaching positions.

You can produce the CV in Word with a picture or logo inserted. You can print it or e-mail it. When I first started my business, I sought professional help from a graphic designer. As I became more comfortable with design, I was able to do something as simple as a CV myself.

Brochures

Now, let's take a look at other promotional material for an individual entrepreneur or business owner. In describing business services, a one-page or brochure is appropriate. We are seeing less need for brochures, however, because most businesses have a Web site.

Figure 7.4 is an example of a one-page description of services from the Fantastic Sam's Web site. It's clear from reading the description that they provide a complete line of services for the hair and a line of salon products.

At Fantastic Sam's Salons, the real question should probably be: *What don't we do?*

Our goal is to make each customer look and feel fantastic. We offer lots of services, like haircuts and styles, up-dos, straightening, coloring, highlights, and texturizing. We also offer beard and mustache trims, and facial waxing, as well as rejuvenating hair treatments for stressed or damaged hair. Our stylists are professionals who are always up-to-date on the latest styles and trends. So we guess you could say that keeps us on the cutting edge!

And so you can get that fresh-from-the-salon look every day, Fantastic Sams also offers our own line of salon products. Our exclusive brand includes shampoos, conditioners, and styling aids that are specially formulated with our own FantasticComplex™, which strengthens, smoothes, and adds shine to hair. Best of all, our line offers you salon products at a fraction of what products at other salons cost.

Whether it's with our salon services or our line of products, Fantastic Sam's gets you looking good, and feeling good about how affordable we are!

Figure 7.5: Fantastic Sam's one-page description.

This one-page could be turned into a brochure that would have a description of the services, the employees, perhaps the prices, and the location and times of services. Think Who, What, When, Where, Why, and How. The "Why" would be the benefits to the consumer as listed in the brochure.

In figure 7.5, the benefits appear to be the affordable price, the variety of services and products, and the improved look and condition of your hair. I'm sure that the convenience of a location would also have an influence on purchasing these services.

Success Stories

Although businesses have used endorsements or success stories for a number of years to promote their businesses, I may be the first career counselor to suggest that success stories be used for entrepreneurs and to promote individual job seekers. They look great when mailed with a resume or CV and business card inside a two-pocket portfolio, which you can buy at any office-supply store. Success stories give you the extra room for more information than you can include in a resume or CV. They help prepare you for an interview.

Within the last two years, success stories in the form of endorsements are also being included in job seekers' and entrepreneurs' profiles on LinkedIn (www.linkedin.com), which has become known as the premier business-networking site.

Figure 7.6 shows how you can format your success stories. You can either write them about yourself or your business, or solicit testimonials from satisfied clients. And by the way, when you write them about yourself or compile your endorsements, you will feel 100 percent better about yourself. Notice that each success story contains a headline, as you might find in a news release.

Success Stories for Andrea Bartlett

Andrea Bartlett selected by American Management Association to teach presentation skills.
Andrea Bartlett was selected by the AMA to teach presentation skills in Atlanta, Chicago, and New York beginning in September 2009. She was chosen from a field of 100 candidates.

Andrea Bartlett selected by Kennesaw College to teach Continuing Education for teachers. Ms. Bartlett will be teaching **Drama Techniques for Teachers** on Saturday, July 14, 2008, from 9 a.m. to 4 p.m.

A. Bartlett achieves Silver International Toastmasters Award. "I am so proud of Andrea," said John Mixon, the President of Speaker's Roundtable, a Decatur Club. "She is a high achiever, a great speaker, and a true asset to our club."

Andrea Bartlett named teacher of the year at Decatur High School.
On May 5, 2008, Andrea Bartlett was named teacher of the year at Decatur High School. Although this was only her second year of teaching, Andrea was nominated and chosen for this award by a committee of students and faculty for her innovative approach to teaching junior and senior English classes and speech and drama.

Ms. Bartlett directs winning drama team in Regional One-Act Play Contest.
Bartlett says that last week's win (March 2007) was a team effort. She had wonderful students to work with. "Practicing the *Wall-to-Wall War* was exciting for the students. It's a very physical play with a serious message that all of us can relate to. We had tough competition, but we gave it our all and won."

Contact Andrea at 770-892-2228 or andrea@website.com

Figure 7.6: Sample success story sheet.

If you look at these success stories, they are not exactly Olympic gold medals but grouped together they show a track record of teaching and presenting achievement that has helped Andrea build her speaking and training career.

Web Sites

Now let's take a look at some of the characteristics of a successful Web site:

- It is simple and easy to navigate.
- It has visual appeal, and sometimes vocal appeal in terms of video or music.
- It uses an attention-getting device, such as quotations, music, pictures, or video.

- It is appropriate and professional.

- It is consistent within itself and with all other promotional material.

- It is easy to understand. It makes it easy to get in touch with the entrepreneur and his business and easy to order and pay for products and services.

- It ranks high in search engines when customers search for particular keywords.

Unless you have Web-design skills, you will probably need to outsource the design and development of your site. Choosing a webmaster should involve more than a telephone interview. The individual should be recommended to you by another customer. You should meet him or her in person if possible to see whether the chemistry is there. You should view the Web sites he or she has designed and hosted.

I have a mature Web site, www.atlantacareertransition.com. It costs me in the neighborhood of $1,000 a year to maintain, upgrade, and pay for credit-card processing. But the benefits are worth it. At least a third of my business comes from Internet searches. For the other two thirds, I use the site as a brochure to walk potential clients through my services and the process. And, because clients can pay for services on the Web site, I am able to collect my fees before I meet with my clients. There are no accounts-receivable issues in my business.

Following are two sites to look at that meet all of the AAAACC criteria, plus are easy to navigate and searchable:

- www.leebryanid.com: Interesting music and visual effects, appropriate for an interior designer.

- www.nsiteful.com: Look at my webmaster's site for many representative Web sites.

Always look at your competition's Web sites and you'll know what you are up against.

Product Packaging

Many people starting a business will skimp on product packaging, but like every other piece of promotional material the packaging should meet the AAAACC standards and represent you in the best way possible. Say no to homemade packaging.

Putting It All Together

Many people starting their businesses are on a limited budget and do not have total clarity as to the products and services they will ultimately offer. In this first year, it is fine to go with moderate-cost promotional material and buy in small quantities until your business is clarified.

When I first began my business, I ordered my cards from www.vistaprint.com. Before that, I printed my own business cards on the computer. Also, at one time I had a prefab Web site where I imported my own pictures and wrote my own HTML. These pre-fab sites will work like online business cards for you, but it is unlikely that they will show up well in Google searches or support online sales processing, so go with a professional webmaster to design a few really good pages.

As you grow in your business and your income increases, you can continue to upgrade your promotional material. It is better to get started than to wait on the sidelines until you achieve perfection. This will never happen.

Web sites, business cards, and letters are all part of your professional image and present a positive, neutral, or negative impression about you and your business. Your self-presentation can also present a positive, neutral, or negative statement about you. In fact, my image consultant Peggy Parks (www.parksimagegroup.com) stresses that creating a positive visual and vocal impression will increase a job seeker's salary and an entrepreneur's business income.

CHAPTER 8

Strategic Searches Online and Off

By now you have created or know how to create a *Wow!* resume and awesome promotional material. You also understand how to achieve memorable first impressions while networking and interviewing. Now it's time to put your knowledge to work in strategic searches online and offline. Read on and find out about the merits of looking for jobs in the traditional way and on the Internet; why career counselors recommend using multiple search methods, and how to network your way into a fulfilling second career.

"Don't put all of your eggs in one basket" is part of the wisdom available to you as a mature job seeker. And if you want to shorten your job search and increase your chances of landing a job, "put many eggs in many different baskets" is even better advice. What this means to you in your career search is that if you employ more than one job search method and increase the number of daily contacts to prospective hiring managers and networking contacts, you will exponentially increase the odds of a faster and more fruitful job search.

Effective job search methods include

- Networking on- and offline
- Strategic mailing and calling
- Posting your resume on company Web sites and selected job search portals (such as CareerBuilder)
- Answering newspaper and online ads
- Working with employment agencies, retained search consultants, and executive recruiters

In this chapter, you'll find a wealth of information about each method.

Networking Your Way to a Job

"The percentage of jobs found through networking is about 60 to 80 percent or even higher, according to studies conducted by outplacement firms, executive search firms, and the U.S. Department of Labor."

—Networking for Job Search and Career Success,
Michelle Tullier, Ph.D. (JIST Publishing)

Networking in the job search process means formally or informally letting as many people as possible know that you are in the market for a new job. Some people grimace when they hear the word *networking,* thinking that it means going to a formal networking event and talking to strangers. The good news for you is that networking is often just talking to your friends and normal day-to-day contacts about what is going on in their lives and yours.

Why Should You Network?

There are a number of excellent reasons for networking your way into an interview. First, experts agree that the majority of jobs are landed through networking. In fact, Ellen Sautter, co-author of *Seven Days to Online Networking,* recently shared with me that her research has shown that 40 percent of networking jobs have come from contacts at LinkedIn (www.linkedin.com), a premier online networking site. Another excellent reason for networking in to a hiring manager is that your resume comes in individually with a recommendation. Without networking, your resume joins the pile of 499 resumes from other job seekers.

Here are a few more good reasons to network:

- As a mature client, your advantage is that you have more networking contacts than younger workers. You have former work colleagues, friends, neighbors, relatives, professional associations, clubs, religious organizations, and so on. And you can also network with strangers at formal networking and association events.

- Networking uncovers unadvertised jobs that represent at least 70 percent of open or soon-to-be-open positions. To expand my career consulting business, I networked with a friend at Toastmasters and was referred to Right Management. There I uncovered an unadvertised position. Subsequently, I landed an interview and an adjunct position on Right's career management consulting staff.

- Obtaining a job referral through networking usually increases your value in the eyes of the hiring manager.

- Networking allows your name and resume to go directly to the hiring manager and cuts through the often time-consuming and interview-killing screening or scanning process.

- Many positions are posted on company bulletin boards, which networking contacts can access.

The following illustrations show the difference between networking and responding to an Internet or newspaper ad.

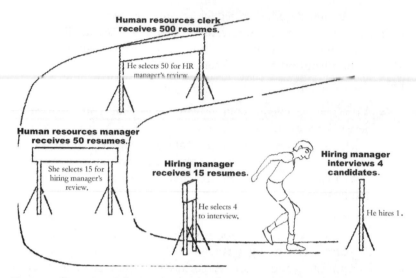

Responding to a job posting over the Internet or in the newspaper.

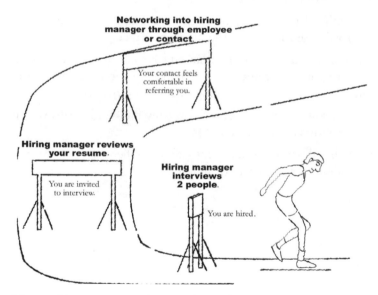

Networking your way into an interview.

Figure 8.1: Jumping the job search hurdles.

You can easily see that networking your way into an interview often delivers your resume directly to the hiring manager. Even if it goes through human resources first, it does not ride in with 499 other resumes. Your resume is given priority because it comes with a referral. It will have even greater credibility if you can persuade your network contact to hand-deliver or attach your resume to a referral e-mail message to the hiring manager.

How Can You Identify Networking Contacts?

As I finished Judy's resume, I asked her how she planned to network. She groaned and said, "I don't think that I have any networks. I have been working at Acme for 20 years. When I wasn't working, I was a full-time mom. I wish I had a Rolodex full of names, but I thought I would retire with Acme. I don't know if I *can* network. I am somewhat introverted. I can't see myself going to these formal networking events."

Judy's feelings are normal. Many career clients recoil when they hear that they need to network. Networking has the bad reputation of being associated with going to meetings and social gatherings where you are forced to "network" with 20 strangers in one hour. I assured Judy that she had more networks than she knew and that networking is a normal daily occurrence. "Once you know what to say about leaving Acme and what you plan to do next, you will find yourself unconsciously networking on a daily basis," I told her.

I presented Judy with the following chart and asked her to write down the names of people that she could contact with ease within the next month.

Who Do You Know?

List one or more people you know in each category that you either normally have interaction with or would be willing to contact within the next month.

Type of Contact	Name, Phone Number, and E-mail	Results
Relatives		
Friends		
Club membership directors		
Club members		
Neighbors		
Former employers		
Former colleagues		
Vendors		
School/college friends		
Clergy		
Common-interest groups		

Professional associations

Competitors

Clients

What Do You Say When You're Networking?

It's easier to call or e-mail your networking contacts when you know what to say to them. Let's take a look at an effective script. Judy agreed to call a former co-worker at Acme who had joined a competitor two years earlier.

- **Identify yourself and give the person a memory connection:** "John, this is Judy Forester. We used to work together at Acme. I was the IT manager. Do you have a moment?"

- **Ask how he or she is doing:** "Are you enjoying your work at Write Image?" (If you were networking with a stranger at a business meeting, you might ask, "Did you enjoy the speaker?")

- **Ask about his or her career:** "Are you in human resources now?" (You might ask a stranger this: "What do you do for a living?") Be polite, listen, and show interest in the other person.

- **Tell him or her about your job situation:** "As you may have heard, Acme has gone through a recent reorganization, and I'm taking this time to explore opportunities as an IT manager with another firm." Or "I'm currently transitioning from IT management to e-learning design. I'm looking for a position as an e-learning course designer."

- **Take time to pause:** At this point, your networking partner will probably ask you a few questions and may provide a referral for you. If not, you can say, "Does your company have any opportunities in this area? Who may I contact?" If this does not work out, explore opportunities outside his or her company by asking, "Do you know of any opportunities with your clients or vendors?"

■ **Close when comfortable:** "John, I really enjoyed talking with you. I'll call you tomorrow to get the name and phone number of your IT contact. I really appreciate your time." Exchange business cards. When you call back, ask for a referral, and if you feel comfortable, ask your contact to deliver or forward your resume with a referral.

Table 8.1 outlines the various dos and don'ts of networking.

Table 8.1: Networking Dos and Don'ts

Do	Don't
Have a clear objective: to obtain a referral.	Be overaggressive; do show interest in your networking partner first.
Be brief and considerate of the person's time. Ask whether this is a good time to talk.	Force conversation if the person is extremely busy.
Have a business card announcing your new career objective.	Immediately hand them your resume.
Take the initiative to follow up on the contact.	Expect your networking partner to take the initiative.
Ask the person if you may use his or her name as a referral.	Fail to thank them and let them know of your progress.
After establishing rapport, ask them to deliver or forward your resume.	Impose on a stranger until you build rapport and the person is no longer a stranger.

Networking Online with LinkedIn

Since 2005, job seekers and entrepreneurs have had the benefit of using LinkedIn (www.linkedin.com), the world's largest professional online network. All job seekers and entrepreneurs with Internet service can access a network of 38 million members in 200 countries, including job seekers, employed business professionals, entrepreneurs, recruiters, and companies including all of the Fortune 500 companies.

I'll have to admit that when I received my first invitation to join LinkedIn, I was so busy that I ignored it. I thought it was a social network and I had plenty of social networks. But in 2007, I ardently embraced LinkedIn, establishing my profile and obtaining recommendations; and I added a new picture in 2008. I can happily report that my efforts work and that I have gotten several new clients through LinkedIn. I insist that my career clients not only complete their profiles on LinkedIn, but that they actively use the site for job search networking.

Take a look at a few of the benefits of using LinkedIn and how people use it:

- Internal and external recruiters use LinkedIn to locate job candidates, including job seekers and employed candidates. They are looking for candidates with closely matching credentials and experience. Often they favor those with complete profiles, including testimonials and a photograph, so be sure yours is as complete as possible.

- Job seekers and entrepreneurs use LinkedIn for networking by inviting people with potentially strong networks to join their network. When an individual joins your network, his network becomes yours and your network becomes his. Although you may have a primary network of only 50 individuals, you are likely to have an extended network of 500,000. After two years I have a primary network of 100 and an extended network of 1.9 million people. You will often see a networking contact within your targeted company of interest. LinkedIn then provides a formal online method of connecting with the individual to set up an information interview or request formal networking into the company in which you are interested.

- Additional features on LinkedIn include a job bank as well as professional associations and alumni and special-interest groups. There are new user startup guides that will give you step-by-step information on how to use LinkedIn. An easy-to-use, complete resource for LinkedIn and other online networking sites is *Seven Days to Online Networking* (Sautter and Crompton, JIST Publishing).

Strategic Mailing and Calling Campaigns

I recently sent this e-mail to past participants in my "Age as an Advantage" class:

> Greetings. It has been nearly a year since we were together. I would love to hear from you. I am looking for success stories in the area of strategic searches off- and online.

I received the following e-mail from Richard:

> Gail, I sent out, over time, 250 targeted letters to industries in cities and states where I was willing to live and received a 10 percent positive rate of response of interest, 10 interviews, and a fine job offer that I accepted.

I was intrigued by Richard's e-mail and was interested to learn about how he conducted his strategic mailing and calling campaign. Read on to find out what he did. But first, read about why this method can work for you.

Figure 8.2: Negative Stereotype: Over-40 workers resist change.

Why Should You Conduct a Strategic Mailing and Calling Campaign?

Does just the thought of networking send you into a panic? Are most of your opportunities halfway across the United States? Along with using LinkedIn, you may be a prime candidate for conducting a strategic mailing and calling campaign. Take a look at some major reasons for launching your own campaign:

- A strategic mailing campaign can be less intimidating than personal networking. You can do it by e-mail, by regular mail, and through telephone follow-up.

- Your time commitment is less significant than it is for in-person networking.

- You can conduct the initial part of your campaign without leaving your home and without dressing for success.

- A properly conducted mailing and calling campaign makes you seem "sales savvy."

- You are tapping into the unadvertised job market as you would in networking.

- Less-experienced or unenergetic job seekers do not usually bother to do this because it involves strategic planning.

- If you are a mature worker with mid- to senior-level experience, you will stand out from the crowd.

How Do You Conduct a Strategic Mailing and Calling Campaign?

Richard was a savvy career-transition client who decided to leave no stone unturned. He extensively networked, searched the Internet, and conducted a strategic mailing and calling campaign. Following are the steps Richard took in his strategic mailing and calling campaign.

Step 1: Create a targeted business list.

Use the Internet or the library to create a targeted business mailing list. Compile this list by industry, city, and state or county. If your list is too long, you can further define it by number of company employees. Your search may reveal your contact person, the hiring manager (such as the director of finance or the vice president of sales and marketing); or you may have to go to the company Web site or make a telephone call to obtain this information. If you are in out-placement or working with a career counselor, you may have access to online databases such as Dun and Bradstreet or Hoovers. If you don't have access, try these alternatives:

- **CorporateInformation** (www.corporateinformation.com): Covers businesses worldwide. The most comprehensive reports come from its Global Professional Services Lists. The subscription costs $575 per year.

- **Hoovers** (www.hoovers.com): A subscription-only database that provides similar information to CorporateInformation and even more, depending on the level you purchase. You can contact Hoovers at 800-281-9173 for pricing information. Recently Hoovers had an introductory offer of 200 free individual business reports.

- **Forbes** (www.forbes.com): Allows you to create a list of the top 2,000 global companies sorted by location or other criteria. You can even create a list of companies that are hiring. This service is free, but your list will contain only basic information. You will need to add your own research from the corporate Web site.

I recommend that you create a list that will keep you occupied for a month. According to Richard, he could send out letters to and call back about 40 contacts a week, so his original list contained 160 companies. (Most people are not this aggressive.)

I recently ran a search for a client, John, in the advertising industry in Chicago, and came up with a list of 87 companies, contacts, addresses, phone numbers, Web sites, and so on. I recommended to John that he stagger his mailing by sending out 25 to 30 letters per week and calling them the following week, at the rate of five per day.

Step 2: Verify your contact information before creating your letters.

Even if you buy business lists, you cannot be assured that the executive you planned to contact is still in place. Always look on the company Web site or call to verify the appropriate contact. As we all know, executives change companies frequently. Here are two tips for getting more information:

- Ask for an executive profile when you call to verify contact information. This will give you customized information to include in your letter and help in your interview.

- Look for current news stories in your database or on the company Web site for additional custom information to use in your letter and in the interview.

Step 3: Create an attention-getting letter.

The most influential book I have read about marketing to executives is *Selling to VITO* (Anthony Parinello, Adams Media). *Selling to VITO* addresses how to sell yourself and your services to a *very important top officer*. My clients and I have successfully used the principles in this book to attract interest and achieve our call objectives. These are the key principles I have adopted from the book:

- Begin your letter with a statement about yourself in bold italics. It could be your own comment about yourself or a strong testimonial about you from a former employer. An example would be

  "Scott Dumas consistently exceeds annual sales goals in all economic conditions, and he is an exemplary motivator for the sales troops." —Lucas Solard, Sr. Vice President, Motion Industries

- Use the contact person's first name in your greeting. For example, use "Dear Patricia" instead of "Dear Ms. Jones." This may seem overly bold to those of you who were taught never to go on a first-name basis until asking for permission. But, quite frankly, the "asking for first-name permission" rule of business address is passé unless you are recently out of college, in your 20s, or addressing a political figure or someone who is always called by their title. By getting on a first-name basis in your letter, you project higher self-esteem and establish yourself on equal footing with the person to whom you are writing. I can say with great assurance that this method is effective in business correspondence.

- Include benefits to the employer in the body of the letter. Use easy-to-read bullets. If I were an administrative assistant, I might say that my strengths include the ability to be immediately productive in a fast-paced environment; recognized for tact and diplomacy under fire; highly skilled in Word, Excel,

Peachtree Accounting, and PowerPoint; consistent team build-er; and team player.

- Mention when you will call back in the closing sentence of your letter. For example, use "I will call back on Thursday, May 21st, at 10:00 a.m. to discuss the possibility of meeting with you in person at a mutually convenient time." It is important to suggest the exact date and time for the potential telephone appointment. Of course, the addressee may be unavailable at the suggested appointment time, but your letter and callback show the seriousness of your approach. The reception to this approach was so favorable that one of my clients actually had an administrative assistant call her to reschedule the telephone appointment.

Following is an example of a letter using the *Selling to VITO* approach.

"Susan is the most outstanding supervisor I have ever worked with. She has consistently exceeded our expectations in customer service and cost savings."

—*Don Jones, Vice President of Marketing, AAA Life*

Dear Richard,

Thank you very much for your time and consideration.

After more than 10 years of successful experience in life insurance and variable annuity administration, I am seeking a supervisory position in customer relations where I can contribute my strengths in

- Customer conflict resolution and retention
- Significant cost savings through attention to detail
- In-depth knowledge in life insurance and variable annuities

As you can see from the attached resume, my record is one of increasing responsibility. I am interested in exploring with you how my background might benefit your organization.

I will telephone you next Thursday, December 5, at 10:00 A.M. to discuss opportunities within your organization.

Sincerely,

Susan Kote-Tawia

Figure 8.3: Sample letter using the "Selling to VITO" approach.

Always direct your letter to the highest available hiring manager. For example, after researching the company, an accountant might direct her correspondence to the chief financial officer or controller.

Remember that the object of your cover letter is to positively attract interest so that your follow-up call receives a positive response. The positive response can be an interview; learning that this business is not hiring now, but will be in six months; finding out you are not qualified for the position; or getting a lead to another company. A negative response is that your phone calls are never returned, which does occasionally happen. This response does not mean that they will never be interested; just that they are not interested right now. So feel free to call again.

Step 4: Send out a week's mailing with staggered callback dates.

Richard sent out 40 letters a week and was able to call that many people back. He did not include the date and time on his letter, but he did indicate he would call back early the next week. His approach was good in that he did not rely on them to call him back. An even stronger approach is to state the date and time you will call them back.

When I first started my business, I sent out a staggered strategic mailing to 100 corporations. I found that I could call only 25 a week. I blocked off specific days and times in my calendar to call back and left other time free to be out of my office. What happened after the first week was that my call activity began to mushroom. Like Richard, I found my success rate to be 10 percent in terms of interest, and ultimately 50 percent in terms of actual business from the 10 percent of interested companies.

Step 5: Call your contacts back at the designated time and don't give up.

When Richard and I began calling back, we frequently got voice mail or an administrative assistant. Following are the tips we share:

- **If you get the assistant, ask for the executive by their first name.** You will frequently be put through.

- **Explain to the assistant the purpose of your call.** For example, "This is Richard Cohen. I mailed John my resume last week and would like to speak to him briefly if I may." If the assistant screens you, establish a telephone appointment with the executive and build rapport with the assistant.

- **When you get voice mail, leave a brief message.** "This is Susan Kote-Tawia. I mailed you my resume last week. I am calling to establish a convenient time to speak to you on the telephone to discuss opportunities within your company. Please call me back at (878) 504-3299. I will be available all afternoon and tomorrow morning before noon."

- **Don't give up.** Follow up, but don't overdo it. If you don't get a return call, try calling on different days and at different hours. One of my career applicants secured an interview and landed a new career after leaving eight voice mails with the hiring manager spaced out over two months. She finally got her contact on the ninth call.

- **It is a good idea to intersperse voice mail with other types of contact, such as a postcard, article of interest, and so on.** Statistically, an individual needs to hear about you five different times in order to make a buying decision, which begins with an interview. Varying your method of contact encourages your rate of success and keeps you from being a pest.

- **Reward yourself for making your calls on time.** I have always rewarded myself with a lunch, frozen yogurt, or an exercise outing after I have finished my calls.

- **Reward yourself whether you reach your executive contact in person or reach voice mail.** Reward your consistency. The results of your efforts will pay off!

Table 8.2: Strategic Mailing and Calling Dos and Don'ts

Do	Don't
Mail to the top hiring manager.	Mail to no name, wrong name, or HR Director unless requested to do so.
Include an exciting heading.	Send a ho-hum letter.
Describe benefits for the employer.	Be self-serving.
Call back as indicated in the letter.	Send so many letters that you know you cannot possibly make all the calls.

Use your networking script when you call back.	Be unprepared when you call back or expect them to call you.
Stay optimistic. It's a matter of numbers, time, and attitude.	Give up.

Effective Online Searches

Career counselors see many career-transition clients whose idea of online career search is limited to posting their resume on dozens of online job boards such as Monster and CareerBuilder. Five reasons that this online method is generally ineffective are

- Millions of resumes are posted on Monster and CareerBuilder.

- The job postings are not always updated or removed.

- At least 70 percent of job opportunities are not listed on these sites.

- Many executive jobs and certain industry jobs are never listed online.

- Spending all day in front of a computer posting on multiple job banks is inefficient and can be depressing. Instead, you can focus your attention on one of two aggregators: Indeed (www. indeed.com) or Simply Hired (www.simplyhired.com). Using either site, you will be able to view the majority of job postings on all other job banks.

- You can use portals such as CareerBuilder as a source of general career information. CareerBuilder is a comprehensive site that allows you to post your resume on its job bank and also offers advice and resources. It's tailored to all but senior-level executive positions.

Searching on the Internet can be an effective tool if you know which Web sites to use and how to use them.

> ### Jerry: Using Online Resources Effectively
>
> I heard Jerry speak at a networking event about his online success and scheduled an interview with him. Jerry, age 48, landed a position as a software engineer with a major newspaper in slightly over four months, thanks to his Internet savvy and his strong interpersonal skills. He also received an increase over his former salary as a software engineer for a national bank.
>
> I wanted to know firsthand why he was staying in software engineering and how he conducted his Internet research. He had a potential age issue, and his reason for leaving the bank was that his position migrated overseas. Jerry told me that he was staying in a volatile field because he felt that organizations would always have quality and coordination issues that would need to be addressed locally and not overseas. He felt that in a few years, he would be even more valuable because increasing problems would surface with overseas IT employment.

Why Should You Conduct an Online Search?

After talking with Jerry about the results of his online search for employment, I am convinced that working online is a useful tool for every job search: for company, position, and salary research; for posting resumes at selected portals and company Web sites; and for communicating with hiring managers and other contacts where e-mail is appropriate. (E-mail is appropriate in IT and telecommunication contacts, networking, and responding to openings when requested in this fashion. But never underestimate the power of a beautiful letter and resume on high-quality stationery.)

Although networking is usually credited with being the most effective job search method, I am seeing opposite indications from companies that are reporting that their major hiring comes through their own Web sites or through LinkedIn. So an effectively conducted Internet job search is certainly worth the time and effort.

How Should You Conduct an Online Search?

Jerry's experience proves that a resourceful person can conduct a successful job search campaign by thoughtful use of the Internet. I found the following how-to tips to be true about online job searches:

- Use LinkedIn for online networking.

- Locate position openings on Simply Hired and Indeed.

- Consider using ExecuNet (www.execunet.com) and The Ladders (www.theladders.com), subscription Web sites for executive-level positions.

- Use CareerBuilder as a comprehensive site for entry-level through mid-level positions.

- Post your resume on the sites of executive recruiters, employment agencies, and retained search firms.

- Keep your resume updated online and resubmit it twice a month.

- Follow up your Internet posting by sending your *Wow!* resume and dynamic cover letter to the hiring manager by snail mail.

The bottom line is that you can find and attract an employer by sending your resume through a job portal or through the company's Web site. But what will sell the employer is your self-presentation, which includes your written resume and cover letter and how well you interview.

Even when you are conducting an online search, you must develop your interpersonal skills. When I heard Jerry speak to our networking group, I thought, "No wonder this guy found a job so quickly. He has an excellent sense of humor and good timing. He is a great storyteller and could be a standup comedian." When you hear Jerry and are with him, you feel that he would fit in culturally with most organizations and would be enjoyable to work with. He certainly overcomes the negative stereotype that mature workers are a cultural misfit.

Table 8.3: Dos and Don'ts of an Internet Job Search

Do	Don't
Be selective in your Internet posting.	Spend all your time in front of a computer screen.
Repost your resume every two weeks.	Leave your resume up forever without reposting.
Follow your Internet posting with a hard copy of your resume and cover letter.	Rely only on your Internet written presentation.
Apply on company Web sites and selected portals.	Plaster your resume on all job boards and include your Social Security number on your resume.
Use current keywords and submission requirements.	Disregard keywords in your resume and submission requirements.
Determine whether your position and industry are suited to an Internet job search.	Rely on the Internet as your only job search method.

Answering Ads in the Newspaper

Never underestimate the power of a local newspaper, such as the *Atlanta Journal and Constitution,* or a national newspaper, such as the *Wall Street Journal,* for locating a job. Although this may seem to be a low-tech approach, it has a higher success rate than large Internet job boards—some sources say as high as 12 percent. And many newspapers also post these ads on their own Web sites. Newspaper ads are usually for entry-level to medium-range positions, with the exception of the *Wall Street Journal,* which posts senior- and executive-level positions. Neighborhood newspapers are a good source for local jobs.

Table 8.4 includes some dos and don'ts for answering newspaper ads.

Table 8.4: Dos and Don'ts for Answering Newspaper Ads

Do	Don't
Apply for the job if it is a close match.	Apply for the job if the match is questionable.
Answer the ad late in the first week to avoid the crowds.	Answer the ad on Monday with the rest of the world.
	Respond to the ad the way that you choose instead of the requested way.

Partnering with Others in Your Job Search

In the mid-90s, employment agencies, retained search firms, and executive recruiters were a "no-sweat" way to manage your job search without having to network heavily, do strategic mailing and calling, or spend time looking at ads.

Employment agencies, retained search firms, and executive recruiters remain excellent resources, but because of the growth of the Internet, many companies employ them less in order to save money. Companies are relying instead on their own internal recruiters and Web sites to attract candidates. (The exception is in the search for key executive positions such as Chief Operating Officer, where executive recruiters and retained search firms are frequently employed.)

Your personal situation determines whether you should research and contact employment agencies, retained search firms, and recruiters. Read on to find why and when, as well as the dos and don'ts of working with job search firms and individuals.

Before we proceed, I want to give you this caveat: Beware of scams. I have recently had two clients who paid between $2,500 and $6,000 up front to a business that claimed to guarantee job results. These clients received inferior resumes, outdated business lists, and mass mailings of their resume with an ineffective cover letter. My clients diligently followed up on their resume mailings with no positive results and were desperate when they came to see me. You've heard the adage, "If something appears too good to be true, it probably is." This applies to the job search assistance business.

What Do You Need to Know About Using an Employment Agency?

Of all the groups you can hire to help you find a job, contingency employment agencies have the most job listings, and the employer pays them a fee only if they fill the position. There is no charge to you. Keep the following three points in mind as you consider using a contingency agency:

- Use contingency agencies if you have an easily classified position, such as staff accountant, administrative assistant, or insurance claims adjuster.

- You can locate contingency agencies in the *Yellow Pages* or online under Employment Agencies in your city. Also, most states have an association of personnel consultants. Georgia's, for example, is the Georgia Association of Personnel Services (GAPS).

- Choose employment agencies that specialize in your position and your industry. For example, MATRIX Resources (www. matrixresources.com) is a firm that offers staffing solutions to the IT industry.

What Do You Need to Know About Using a Retained Search Consultant?

Retained search consultants charge a retainer to fill specific corporate positions for a defined period of time. Again, there is no fee involved for you. Retained search consultants usually conduct their own search of candidates and do not actively encourage job seekers to contact them except to post a resume on their Web sites. You may get lucky and catch their attention and you may be able to network your way into their firms to create special notice. Be aware of the following points when considering using these retained search consultants:

- Respond to retained search consultants when they approach you. Treat your interview seriously.

- If you are highly compensated and have impeccable experience in a senior corporate management position, approach retained search consultants through their Web sites or a networking contact.

- A few of the well-known firms are Korn/Ferry International; Heidrick and Struggles, Inc.; and SpencerStuart.

What Do You Need to Know About Using an Executive Recruiter?

Executive recruiters are usually paid on a fee basis, which represents a percentage of the candidate's first-year salary. Again, there is no cost to you. Executive recruiters usually are more interested in finding you than having you contact them because they have specific positions to fill. However, if recruiters have strong contacts with major firms and your current position is in demand, they may be willing to champion your cause—especially if you have provided them with referrals in the past.

Following are a few tips for working with executive recruiters:

- Use executive recruiters if they approach you. Treat interviews with them seriously.

- If you have impeccable experience in senior management or a high-demand position, you can approach executive recruiters through their Web sites or through networking.

- To find executive recruiters, see the Executive Search Firms page on The Riley Guide at www.rileyguide.com/firms.html.

Table 8.5: Dos and Don'ts of Hiring Others to Conduct Your Job Search

Type of Service	Do Approach If You	Don't Approach If You
Employment agency	Have an easily classified position that is in demand and a solid track record of consistency and achievement.	Are making a dramatic career change; have a difficult-to-classify position, spotty work history, or low achievement history.
Retained search firm	Are a highly compensated, marketable senior executive with a solid, consistent track record of achievement.	Are entry- to mid-level; not highly compensated; and not marketable because of your position, industry, inconsistent work history, or poor track record of achievement.
Executive recruiter	Are well compensated and marketable; mid- to senior level; with a solid, consistent track record of achievement.	Are not well compensated or marketable; entry level; or without a solid, consistent track record of achievement.
Temporary and contract employment agencies	Look for agencies that specialize in your position or industry. These jobs are a great filler and a good way to find a new job.	Expect to make your normal salary or get perfect assignments.

Organizing Your Search

Whether you use one or multiple job search methods, organizing your efforts is critical. In no time, you will have applied for multiple positions through networking, over the Internet, through newspaper ads, in mailing campaigns, and so on, and the calls will start coming in. If you are not organized, one day you will get a phone call from an HR professional or hiring manager and have no recall of the company, the hiring manager, or the position. This very bad feeling is one that you want to avoid.

You can easily organize your job search using an alphabetized accordion folder and filing information by company. I personally prefer the accordion folder to an index-card box because the folder will hold your letters, ads, postings, company research, and so on. Keep this folder by your telephone. You can establish a callback diary by using an ACT software program, an Excel spreadsheet, Outlook Express, or a simple filing system of employers to call on Monday through Friday. This could be a card index system; or even easier, keep one folder open in your accordion system for next-day calls.

A helpful hint for staying on track is to set daily networking, calling, and mailing goals. Preparing these goals and pulling supporting information the afternoon or night before you call allows you to sleep soundly, feel refreshed, and get started early the next morning. A bonus is that the right side of your brain processes these contacts overnight and helps you be more creative.

Choosing Your Strategic Search Methods— Online and Off

No two career candidates are alike, and their search methods should not be alike, either. Here's what I mean:

- A 52-year-old senior retail management client found her position through networking. She never searched online, never used a retained search firm, and never did a strategic mailing and calling. She instinctively knew that networking was the way to go for her position in the retail industry and her target companies were limited.

- On the other hand, a 48-year-old software engineer found his position online but also networked on the side. He hedged his bets by using two job search methods that were both appropriate for his position and his industry.

- And then there's the 57-year-old telecommunications sales manager who networked, posted his resume online, worked with executive recruiters, and then landed an outstanding position by initiating a strategic e-mail campaign to key executives. He used all methods appropriately and simultaneously.

There is no one-size-fits-all approach to job searching. Choose the approaches that best fit your position, industry, personality, and age. As a rule, networking on- and offline is an excellent approach for mature candidates. Strategic mailing and calling also works. The Internet can be productive if your position is among those frequently posted. The newspaper can be effective for frequently posted and unusual, seasonal, and part-time positions. Retained search firms and executive recruiters love highly compensated senior managers but will often hesitate to represent anyone 60 or older. Employment agencies, both permanent and contract, can be helpful for specific industries for positions under senior management.

And remember that there is always the "strange attractor" or the unique way that you can present yourself that works for you and hasn't even been discovered. One of my clients discovered his last position on the bulletin board of his church. This was the only place the position was posted.

The more employers hear about you in multiple ways—such as getting a letter, getting a phone call, hearing about you from a referral, and so on—and the more types of search methods you employ, the greater the chances that you will be successfully employed.

What Job Search Methods Will You Use?

Take a moment to select the job search methods that you are willing to explore and then make a few notes on how you plan to approach each opportunity.

❑ Networking on- and offline

_____

_____

❑ Strategic mailing and calling

_____

_____

❏ Online searching

_____

_____

❏ Searching in the newspaper

_____

_____

❏ Partnering with others (employment agencies and recruiters)

_____

_____

CHAPTER 9

Achieve Memorable First Impressions and Ace Interviews

Ifirst met Teresa, a potential career transition client, over the phone and was impressed with the ease of our conversation. We set an appointment to meet the following Monday and Teresa sent her resume by e-mail for my review. She was a high school English teacher and wanted to transition into insurance adjusting. Her resume was good, not awesome, but I could tell by her education, experience, and achievements that she was a high achiever. I looked forward to our meeting.

Teresa was dressed in a well-fitting navy blue suit accented by medium-height, stylish, closed-toe, navy leather heels. She carried a black portfolio and wore simple gold jewelry. Her brown hair was stylishly cut and she wore what have become called Sarah Palin–style glasses. She walked energetically to meet me, looked me straight in the eye, shook my hand firmly and warmly, and said, "Gail, it's a pleasure to meet you. Thank you so much for taking the time to meet with me today." Her voice was clear, pleasant, and not over-loud. I thought to myself, "So far, so good. Great first impression. Let's see what this woman has to offer."

A wise person once said, "You never have a second chance to make a first impression."

In this chapter, you'll find out how to create a dynamic personal advertisement composed of attractive visual and vocal components that will result in an interview; a referral; a job offer; or in the case of an entrepreneur, a sale of product or services. And after you've learned how to make a memorable first impression, I'll cover how to give awesome answers to tough interview questions.

The Importance of the First 60 Seconds

First impressions are formed within the first 60 seconds of meeting someone and are made up primarily of visual cues and vocal energy. Visual cues account for 55 percent of what people believe; vocal energy accounts for 38 percent; and information, only 7 percent.

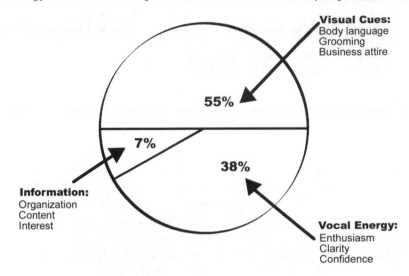

Because a memorable, standout first impression is created in an extremely short period of time, it's critical for you to send positive visual and vocal cues that say, "I'm friendly, self-confident, intelligent, energetic, and people savvy." I have never met a serious career transition client who wanted to deliberately send a message that says, "I'm unfriendly, have low self-esteem, have low physical and mental energy, and am not interpersonally sensitive." Those negative visual and vocal messages are usually sent because job seekers and entrepreneurs are unaware of how they are being perceived by their interviewer, networking partner, or potential buyer.

Although it's true that first impressions can be strengthened or corrected during the interview or networking conversation, it's hard to overcome a strong negative first impression. If you want people to believe the best about you, you must show them before you tell them.

Recognize That You Are the Product: Your Presence Is the Advertisement

Do you know that you are your product, and the first impression that you create is your ad? My brother and I sold our mom's house. Here is the core text we used on the real-estate flyer:

> Charming 3-bedroom, 2-bath ranch-style home in the highly desirable Silver Hills neighborhood. Completely updated kitchen and baths. Recent master bath addition with spacious bedroom, bath, and walk-in closet.

Before the house was renovated, a "deadly" honest ad would have read like this:

> Fifty-year-old ranch-style home for sale in once-desirable neighborhood. Kitchen and baths have original appliances and fixtures. Beware of the basement, which has rickety steps and occasionally floods in a heavy rain.

Which ad do you think would attract more buyers and most effectively support the price we wanted for our home? Writing the original less-than-enticing ad for our home was a joke, but it led us to the conclusion that we needed to renovate the older ranch.

When it came time to show our home, I played to the buyer's five senses with visually attractive home staging both inside and curbside. The staging, using my own furniture and accessories, was inexpensive. The house and the yard were spacious and uncluttered. Flowers bloomed in the window boxes and on the porch. Soft cinnamon scent filled the house interior. Fresh paint and new appliances and fixtures were part of the renovation. Needless to say, the buyers loved it and the house sold.

If we had posted the enticing ad, which correlates to your writing the best resume and cover letter possible, but left the house as-is, what a difference! Potential buyers viewing the home would have discovered that their on-site impression was not consistent with our written ad; the house would not have sold for a fair price, it would have been on the market longer, or we might be still be paying utilities and taxes on an empty house.

When you write the best *Wow!* resume possible and consistently create and present a positive interview and networking personal appearance, you too will sell yourself more quickly for top dollar.

On the other hand, if you elect to present yourself "as-is" and "as-is" looks outdated, frumpy, slumpy, and unenergetic, you will be perceived as unattractive. Your product, You Inc., will not sell on the market quickly for top dollar and your career search or career change will stall.

In the next few sections, I will share with you the key elements that positively affect an interview and networking first impression. In order to create a vivid, positively memorable impression, you as a career client or entrepreneur—like a home seller—must also appeal to the senses by offering an image that looks good, sounds good, smells good, and feels good. Fortunately, you do not have to be concerned about tasting good.

The Key Elements That Positively Affect First Impressions

The key elements that positively affect interview and networking first impressions are these:

- Erect posture and confident, energetic body movements
- A dynamic, enthusiastic, clearly understood voice
- A clean and properly groomed appearance
- Appropriate and stylish business attire
- A relaxed, centered composure

Let's take a look at each element and find out how it relates to your sensual impression and how you can use it to your advantage.

Use Erect Posture and Confident, Energetic Movements

When a career candidate vigorously walks into my office with head held high, smiles sincerely with full eye contact, and firmly shakes my hand, I am favorably impressed. Wouldn't you be? A vigorous walk with head held high signals energy and self-confidence.

On the flip-side, a tentative walk with poor posture signals low energy and insecurity, and makes me think of Frasier's dad on the sitcom *Frasier*. When you walk energetically with head held high, you are definitely counteracting a potential negative stereotype associated with some older workers, which is that older workers have low energy and may not have the stamina to do the job.

A candidate who makes full eye contact, smiles, and firmly shakes my hand without squeezing so hard that my ring cuts my fingers gets my vote for being confident, energetic, and friendly. That candidate is demonstrating optimism and a positive attitude, recognized as two of the three most important hiring criteria. (The other is aptitude.)

In many ways, your 60-second first impression is an informal test that reveals your optimism or pessimism and a positive or negative attitude. Optimism and a positive attitude are physically revealed in the first 60 seconds of a first impression, whether in person or over the telephone.

"Over 50 companies now use optimistic questionnaires in their selection process to identify people who have not just talent and drive but also the optimism needed for success."

—Learned Optimism, *Martin Seligman*

The combination of smiling, firmly shaking hands, and walking into an office with energy and erect posture is a win-win approach for you that will make a favorable first impression on your interviewer or networking partner. You can elevate their mood *and* your mood, and improve your own position, by using such approach. In the first impression you make, you will have positively influenced the interviewer's visual sense through your smile and erect posture and energetic body movements. And, as a bonus, with your firm, warm handshake, you will have positively appealed to his or her sense of touch.

To Make a Positive First Impression
■ Stand and walk erectly with your head held high.
■ Walk vigorously.
■ Smile sincerely and give direct eye contact.
■ Shake hands firmly.
■ Practice your nonverbal presentation with family and friends; get their feedback.
■ Visualize yourself as a mature runway model.

Project Vocal Energy and Enthusiasm

To project vocal energy and enthusiasm, concentrate on raising the volume of your voice and pace of your speech. Speak a little louder and faster than usual and clearly articulate your words. My caveat (or warning; excuse the former attorney in me) is don't overdo the vocal energy and enthusiasm; don't speak so loudly or talk so fast that you bowl an interviewer over, or you'll create a negative first impression of someone who is inconsiderate, aggressive, and cocky.

Recently, I had a candidate who bowled me over with his voice. He was a 6-foot-4 former basketball player with a booming, almost gruff voice. As his career consultant, I encouraged him to soften his voice, which—combined with his forceful appearance—was intimidating. I was afraid that he would overwhelm a potential employer.

To Project Positive Vocal Energy

- Speak in a moderately loud voice without overwhelming.
- Speak with an energetic pace.
- Clearly articulate your words.
- Smile and speak with enthusiasm.
- Practice with family and friends and get their feedback.
- Tape your greeting and get feedback on your voice.

Polish Your Telephone Voice

Have you ever guessed what a person looked like based on their voice, making assumptions about age, energy, intelligence, and self-confidence? Be honest.

In your career search, your initial 60-second first impression often occurs over the telephone, where vocal tone and energy account for 93 percent of the impression. Interview screenings, networking opportunities, information-gathering calls, and appointment setting are all conducted over the telephone. These phone calls are usually your second opportunity to create a positive first impression after an employer has received your *Wow!* resume and cover letter. So make every effort to reinforce and strengthen your positive first impression with a standout telephone voice.

This means that you must be careful to speak in an upbeat, self-confident voice when you place or answer a call. How can you find out how you sound? Practice sending and receiving prospective interview-related calls with a friend (one who will be honest with you). An interview-related call is a follow-up call to a prospective employer after mailing a cover letter and resume, a call to a networking source to determine the potential for employment in their company, or a true phone screening interview call from a prospective employer or recruiter.

Get feedback on your friend's impression of how you sound. The areas for your friend to evaluate are your vocal delivery and the content of your message. Do you speak in a clear, sincere, warm, and energetic voice? Do you sound prepared but not over-rehearsed? Is your message clear and organized? Are you a good listener?

Another good way to get vocal feedback is to call your own telephone number and leave a 60-second commercial or *elevator speech* (a short, 60-second speech). Critique yourself and then have a friend critique you.

To Create a 60-Second Practice Commercial

- Call a friend or your own voice mail.
- Give a greeting and then ask how the person is doing.
- State your name.
- Share your reason for leaving your last employer or changing careers.
- State the reason for your call.
- Ask for honest feedback.

Can a caller determine your age by your voice? I don't think so unless you sound tired by projecting a soft, slow voice. I can usually judge the age of a young woman because of a higher voice; our voices usually lower with age, but I usually can't guess age unless someone is over 70.

I've had two bizarre telephone turnoffs involving telephone calls to career candidates. One time, a gruff-sounding spouse answered the phone with a growl. I didn't want to call that number again! And then there was the time I called and received a voice mail with scary

Halloween music. Can you imagine a potential employer's first impression of you being created through a gruff spouse or a scary ghoul?

If you're busy or stressed when the phone rings (you're cooking or heading out the door), let the call go into your voice mail so that you can return the call when you're upbeat and prepared to talk to the caller. Never sacrifice the quality of your telephone calls to 24/7 accessibility. This can be tempting if you are accustomed to immediately answering all calls in order to stay connected.

Also, encourage spouses, significant others, and children not to answer your primary contact phone when you're in the job search process. If you want to be totally safe and can afford it, get your own dedicated telephone line or use your cell while you're searching for a job.

Recently, I interviewed Susan Boone, a therapist, about her positive telephone conversation. "How do you always project calmness over the telephone?" I asked. Susan said that she makes a point not to answer the phone on the way out of the door, when she is distracted, or when she does not have time for a short conversation. Letting her calls go into voice mail allows her time to "get her thoughts together." Susan makes it a point to project an emotional feeling of enthusiasm and calmness in her voice.

Prepare a Formal Voice-Mail Message

On more than one occasion, I have been shocked by a career candidate's voice-mail message (or lack of one). Having a professional voice-mail message is important but not difficult. It should be a simple but dignified message such as "This is Ron Swanson. I'm out at the moment, but if you'll leave your name and phone number and a brief message, I'll get back with you shortly."

If you leave your cell phone number on your voice-mail message or use your cell phone exclusively, remember to be upbeat and professional whenever you answer the cell phone.

If you don't have voice mail, you probably are missing out on potential employer calls. When I call a candidate and there is no voice-mail service on the phone, I conclude that this person is not taking their job search seriously. It's not terribly expensive: You can get voice mail from your phone carrier for approximately $5 a month or buy an answering machine for approximately $50.

Caller ID is another telephone feature you might want to explore. It is a real help in knowing when to spontaneously answer the phone and when to let the phone go into voice mail.

According to Norman King, author of The First Five Minutes *(Prentice Hall Press), a lower-pitched voice is associated with self-confidence and integrity. A higher-pitched voice is associated with fear and nervousness. This applies to your voice in person, over the phone, and on your voice mail. Recent surveys have also revealed that we associate faster speech with greater intelligence.*

Your pleasant, enthusiastic voice appeals to an interviewer's sense of hearing. If the interview is over the phone, you can also create a positive visual and emotional image with your voice.

To Create a Winning Vocal First Impression Over the Telephone

- Be prepared for the call.
- Speak enthusiastically with increased vocal volume and pace.
- Practice your 60-second commercial with a friend or through your own voice mail.
- Slightly lower your voice if needed.
- If you are unprepared to receive a call, let it go into voice mail.
- Never sacrifice quality of vocal presentation for accessibility.
- Smile during the conversation to contribute to voice appeal.
- Consider standing up while talking on the phone to create more energy.

Reduce Your Regional or International Accent for Clearer Communication

A regional or international accent can be entertaining and lucrative, if you're given an opportunity to use it in your career. Have you heard Paula Deen, the famous restaurateur from Savannah, use her Southern drawl to promote food or tourism on television? How successful would the *I Love Lucy* TV series have been without Desi's Hispanic accent and his famous line, "Lucy, you've got some 'splainin' to do!"?

Regional and international accents can be charming and don't have to be completely eliminated unless your voice is difficult to understand, grating, or nasal, or you mispronounce and misuse words. If you "murder the king's English," so to speak, or have a totally unpleasant vocal tone, and are hard to understand, your intelligence and professional competence will be discounted.

Although a first impression contains very few words, you will feel more confident in all interviewing and networking situations if you know that you are clearly understood. One of the best ways to "correct" a regional or foreign accent is to record a short narrative or poem and have a trained speaking professional or voice therapist critique your performance and personally work with you.

Some of my clients have chosen to record a poem by Robert Frost called "Fire and Ice" because of its brevity and humor. The poem also contains a number of words that are frequently mispronounced such as "fire" and "twice." Try reading the poem out loud. You can find the text of this poem online at www.bartleby.com/155/2.html. Try reading it out loud.

You can pick up your pace and learn to enunciate correctly by speaking quickly and pronouncing each word clearly. Two short sayings to try are these:

> How much wood would a wood chuck chuck if a woodchuck could chuck wood?

and

> If Peter Piper picked a peck of pickled peppers, how many pickled peppers did Peter Piper pick?

Speaking clearly is a critical part of creating positive interview and networking first impressions. Because our initial impression time is short (60 seconds), make the most of it. Clearly speaking in person and over the telephone will dramatically enhance your vocal presence and positively influence every interview or networking opportunity.

Improve Your Personal Hygiene and Grooming

Bad breath is frequently the result of the beginning of gum disease or illness. Coffee breath and cigarette breath are easier to cure. Don't drink coffee immediately before an interview, and don't smoke a cigarette, which can affect your breath and your clothes. Beware of eating garlic the night before. A good breath check involves licking your tongue on your hand, letting the moisture dry, and smelling your hand. Also, there are two quick ways to improve your breath: drink water or eat an apple.

Check for body odor in your clothes and shoes. Make sure everything you wear is clean. Choose a deodorant that won't fail under interview pressure and networking stress. Antiperspirants work best during stressful times.

Dandruff is easy to cure with an over-the-counter shampoo containing coal tar. Notice your jacket when you take it off. Does it reveal dandruff? Take a look at your glasses. Are they dirty, or do they have dandruff on them?

On rare occasions, I have seen a candidate with extremely wind-blown hair or a slip hanging below her skirt. It helps to arrive early for an interview or networking meeting in time for a last-minute mirror check.

Nails should be clean and well shaped. Clothes should be clean and expertly pressed. Pay attention to all of the small grooming details that give you a "bandbox" look.

As a second-time single woman 20-plus years ago, I wanted to look my personal best and attended Barbizon School of Modeling for a nine-month course. My primary intention was not to become a professional model, but to learn the subtle nuances that would transform me from a slightly frumpy high school teacher to a dynamic, marketable single woman. Although I learned fantastic posture and runway modeling, the most useful information for me came in the form of dressing and dining tips. For instance, most women I know try to match their shoes to the color of their skirt or pants. A more attractive, coordinated look involves matching shoes and stockings, for example, camel suede pumps with stockings close to the same color.

Accessories definitely "punch up" clothing for men and women, such as a colorful man's tie or a woman's scarf. But you have to be careful not to overdo it. For example, wearing rings on many fingers and multiple earrings is considered bad taste. Also, the quality of clothing, shoes, and leather accessories is critical.

I learned that you don't have to be wealthy to be well-dressed. At Barbizon, many of the professional models shopped at designer resale shops, and I have adopted this practice for myself.

The good news is that I landed a wonderful corporate job soon after my graduation from modeling and law school. I learned from the interviewer's comments to me after I was hired that my initial impression was definitely enhanced by my clothing, grooming, and confident presence. Landing a husband took a little bit longer. I was single eight more years.

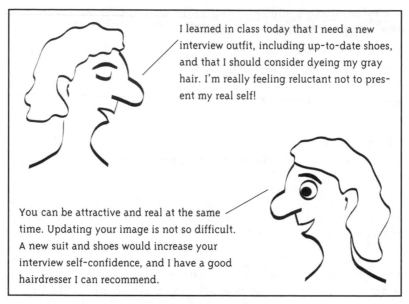

Figure 9.1: Overcoming image-makeover fears.

Choose Appropriate and Stylish Business Dress

Thirty-one years ago John Molloy in *Dress for Success* recognized and capitalized on his version of how the *upwardly mobile executive* should look. Our definition of professional business attire still owes much to his early influence. John Molloy's upwardly mobile executive look later became known as the IBM look and consisted of male and female versions of dark suits, white shirts, and subtly striped or patterned ties or scarves. Today we jokingly refer to people who take this look to extremes as "suits."

You might be so used to business-casual at work that you might not have a formal business suit in your closet, and you might wonder, "What's the fuss over dressing for the interview when the interviewer will be in business-casual and the other employees wear business-casual?" The fuss over dressing in a suit for the interview involves an interview tradition that is centuries old, like the handshake, but was perfected by John Molloy in the late seventies. Unfortunately, interviewers still expect to see candidates wearing a current version of the "dress-for-success" look.

If you don't own a stylish, well-fitting business suit and are on a tight budget, you have several reasonable options which I have used myself. You can

- Shop for a well-fitting suit or dark sport coat at an upscale resale shop.
- Buy a suit or sports coat on sale.
- Borrow a suit or sports coat from a friend.
- Get a free suit from an organization such as Dress for Success (www.dressforsuccess.org).

You announce your serious commitment to the job by wearing appropriate and stylish professional business dress for your interview. You can dress appropriately and stylishly on a very limited budget.

Choose Business Dress with Flair

Despite the fact that the interviewer may be dressed in business-casual, you need to wear the male and female equivalents of a conservative, well-tailored suit in blue, black pinstripe, brown, gray, or camel (women only), but now you can add a colored shirt, shell, or blouse. Men can choose a white or blue shirt and a colorfully patterned tie.

Women can wear a blouse or shell of almost any color except orange. Women can wear a skirted suit; a pants suit works better for mature clients, however, unless they have good legs and are willing to wear stylish but potentially uncomfortable heels. Stockings are always required for an interview despite the sandaled, no stockings, painted-toe look that is popular in warm weather.

Shoes and portfolios should be conservative and of high-quality leather in basic colors. Jewelry and makeup should be minimal but in good taste with a watch and pen of high quality. Strong perfume and cologne are a turnoff.

You can add energy and warmth, or coolness and sophistication, to a business-professional look by using color appropriately. A woman's red blouse and a gray suit can be warm and energizing. A man's blue pinstriped shirt with a blue suit can project coolness and sophistication.

Maine Couple Get Career Makeovers

It is not unusual today to find a couple in career transition at the same time. Such was the case with a couple from Maine who elected to fly down for their career assessment, resume development, and interview practice because they wanted me to comment on their professional appearance and to interview in person. The wife had cautioned me that her husband might need more advice than she might need.

Naturally, I was excited to see them at my front door. We were happy to have them stay in our "guest suite" and work with them over the weekend.

Daniel Before His Executive "First-Impression" Makeover

My first impression of Daniel was striking. He wore very formal business clothes, a blue pinstriped suit, a white shirt, and a red bow tie. Daniel had a black beard and mustache, black hair, and oversized tortoise-shell glasses. He displayed great physical and vocal energy and was well spoken, with a charming British accent. He looked like I would expect a scientist or professor would look. Actually, he was the owner of a software-development company for sale and was looking for an executive-level corporate position. My goal was to make him look like a corporate executive.

Daniel After His Executive "First-Impression" Makeover

After I got to know Daniel better, I suggested appearance changes for him. "Your suit and shirt are fine. While I would rather you adopt a traditional tie, I can live with the bow tie, as it makes you look distinctive. The main changes I suggest are that you remove your beard and trim your mustache. Also, you can order new, more stylish glasses online for under $100." (My husband and I had ordered glasses online and had been satisfied.)

I met with less resistance from Daniel than I expected. Susan, his wife, had probably mentioned appearance changes before, and Daniel wanted a professional confirmation.

Susan Before Her Executive "First-Impression" Makeover

Susan was co-owner of the software company with Daniel. When I first met her, I observed that she had a professional persona. She was well groomed with a very stylish haircut and color. Her makeup was appropriate and her jewelry tasteful. She was wearing glasses that were slightly outdated and her long blazer-style tweed jacket screamed vintage Ralph Lauren. Her physical and vocal energy were excellent. Susan wanted to develop a career in corporate marketing and look younger and more up-to-date.

Susan After Her Executive "First-Impression" Makeover

Susan had only minor changes to make. I complimented her on her cut and color and overall first impression. I suggested that she order new, more stylish glasses and that she buy a shorter-length interview coat or have the one she wore altered. She easily adopted my suggestions.

The happy news is that Dan is now a VP with a software-development company in Seattle and Susan is a paralegal specializing in intellectual property. Their updated first impressions were important components in landing their jobs.

Choose Your Interview and Networking Wardrobe Carefully

When in doubt about your networking and interview wardrobes, just turn to these suggestions, using those that appeal to you or meet your needs:

- Talk to a well-dressed career consultant or an image consultant.

- Observe and present a mature version of a professionally dressed 35- to 45-year-old.

- Look at well-dressed professionals in fashion magazines such as *Instyle* for women and *GQ* for men.

- Consult with your children if they are fashion conscious and knowledgeable.

- If you have definite figure flaws such as waistline bulge or a double chin, get advice on how to use clothing and makeup to minimize these issues.

- Visit a savvy sales professional in a high-end clothing store for advice.

Many of these wardrobe suggestions won't cost you more than your time. You can go to a bookstore and study recent fashion magazines, or seek the advice of a savvy sales professional, even if you don't plan to buy your suit until a later date.

Most importantly, seek out honest advice, not just what you want to hear. Also, make sure that the person giving you the advice is well groomed and fashion conscious. And don't ever wear clothing that is too tight or too large.

You have to be especially vigilant during your career campaign to look your professional best at all times, because you never know when a casual encounter will turn into a job interview. One of my savvy career clients wears makeup on the Stairmaster at her athletic club, because of the extensive networking opportunities she recognizes in that environment. After all, you never know whom you'll run into in the gym, grocery store, or library.

Know When to Wear Business-Casual Attire

Is it ever appropriate for you to wear business-casual attire? Business-casual attire is sometimes appropriate for networking and interviewing *if* business-casual is the "accepted company attire." In some interview sessions, it may be appropriate to wear a blazer and slacks with a turtleneck or open-collared shirt in place of a suit. Company insiders are the best people to advise you whether their company is one of the few in which business-casual would be appropriate for an interview. However, it's smarter to be overdressed in terms of formality for a job interview or networking meeting than to be underdressed in terms of business casual.

Handle Gray Hair with Care

My clients are always asking me about whether to dye their gray hair. Gray hair is usually associated with old age, but we all know that some of us look more distinguished with gray hair than others. And some of us are prematurely gray in our 30s. If you look like the well-known actors James Brolin, also the husband of Barbra Streisand, or Richard Gere, your gray hair is an asset because you are famous and have a young-looking face. If you don't look like Brolin or Gere or the female equivalent, you will not be committing a sin by coloring, highlighting, or lowlighting your hair. Before coloring your hair, it's a good idea to get the opinion of your career consultant, your hairdresser, or an image consultant. You might ask whether you should color your hair, and if so, what shade would look best. Also, you might seek advice on the attractiveness of your haircut. Have your hair professionally colored unless you are already a pro at this.

Recently, one of my career clients asked about dying his mustache. He was balding and didn't have to worry about his hair. I told him to go ahead and dye his mustache, using the special hair color available today for mustache and sideburns that partially covers gray and yet still gives a natural appearance. Why not? What did he have to lose? The next day all the women and men in his career-transition workshop applauded him, because his dyed mustache made him look more vigorous.

Trim Those Beards

Neat, trimmed beards are acceptable if you can't stand to part with them, but the Santa Claus look is out unless you want to be hired for Christmas. If you keep a neatly trimmed beard, it may not be an impediment to landing a job, but be aware that many organizations still harbor distaste for beards. Some people feel that a heavily bearded look is not open and friendly. Beards are more acceptable in education and artistic positions, such a professor, architect, media consultant, and so on.

Beware of Very Long Hair and Teased or Overset Mall Cuts

Very long hair, longer than shoulder-length, on women over 45 presents an outdated look. Longer-than-shoulder-length hair is generally not considered business professional for the younger generation, and on older women the outdated look is magnified. A fresh haircut or putting long hair in a stylish up-do works well. Having outdated, unprofessional hair can reinforce a negative stereotype that you would be a cultural misfit within the organization. Extremely long hair fit in at Woodstock, but is passé in today's business environment.

I once had a talented but snobby hairdresser who referred to highly curled, sprayed, perfectly coiffed hair as "mall cuts." The message that he was sending to me was that contemporary hair should not look perfectly cut, sprayed, and set, but should look natural and a little wind tousled.

Male Hairstyles Matter, Too

Men should wear their hair stylishly short without a ponytail unless they are applying for an artistic endeavor. Too-short hair tends to look like the male equivalent of a "mall cut," so it's a good idea for you to get a haircut the week before, not the week of an important interview or networking meeting. Also, try to avoid an obvious comb-over to cover a balding head.

Professional Hair for Business
■ Professional hair for women is stylishly cut and no longer than shoulder length.
■ Longer hair can be put in a stylish up-do.
■ Professional hair for men is short and stylishly cut.
■ Coloring gray hair, sideburns, beards, and mustaches often presents a more youthful appearance.

Avoid the Danger of Presenting Yourself "As-Is"

At this point, you may be thinking, "Oh, Gail, I just don't want to color or restyle my hair or buy a new business suit. I want to present myself 'as-is.'" I commiserate with you because I've had the same feeling myself. Most Saturday mornings I sleep in, go without makeup, and put on a baseball cap to hide my messy hair. Jeans and a sweatshirt complete my rumpled Saturday look. But I know that in any professional work environment I need to look my professional best, or I lose my credibility as an author, career consultant, and professional speaker.

When you are thinking this way, remember that you can use subtle temporary hair color, have a friend put up your hair, and buy your business suit at a resale shop. You can inexpensively look your best.

If you are strongly resistant to changing your personal image, I recommend that you ask yourself these questions:

- Are you shooting yourself in the foot and eliminating many potential career opportunities by being a nonconformist in small things?

- Why are you opposed to a more youthful or more professional look?

- Are you just being stubborn or lazy?
- What if you love your new look?

Yes, a few employers will take you "as-is," but you may not command top dollar.

Minimize Self-Expressive, Sexy, or Ethnic Dress

In a class I teach on interview techniques, a very articulate corporate trainer expressed her desire to wear African-American dress to networking and interview events. My answer was to suggest that she wear traditional professional business dress with a tribal patterned scarf or self-expressive ethnic pin.

When my clients ask me about wearing self-expressive dress, I can empathize with them. My personal wardrobe consists of a lot of funky and semi-sexy clothes: fur sweaters, flashy rhinestone earrings, and tight black jeans (with Lycra, of course). My personal research, mistakes, and experience confirm that my corporate and career clients will not find me credible if I present a business image that is a combination of a skinny version of Miss Piggy and Dolly Parton. However, I can express myself appropriately by wearing a navy blue business suit, an azalea-pink shell, and a flashy pin of many colored stones.

When you're considering self-expressive dress, ask yourself these questions:

- Is your dress appropriate and stylish business attire for your prospective business environment?
- Are you dressing appropriately for the organizational role that you want to play in the future?
- Are you recognizing and honoring the perception of the interviewer?

Interviewers tend to hire someone who seems like themselves and who appears to fit in culturally within the organization. If your dress doesn't match, you'll be better off to modify it to reflect suitable business attire for that cultural environment.

A few environments seem to tolerate extreme self-expression: artistic environments and behind the scenes in technology and telecommunications, but never in the interview process itself. If personal self-expression is worth that much to you, perhaps self-employment or the entrepreneurial route is your cup of tea.

Face the Fear of Change

Changing your appearance and your dress can be uncomfortable, but personal growth and improvement occur by embracing change. Remember that action precedes feeling. Who's to say that you will not enjoy having brown rather than gray hair or won't fall in love with your new pinstriped suit or your resale blazer?

Can you financially benefit by lowering your voice or buying a new interview suit? Small first-impression changes can definitely energize your career search, and image consultants claim that changes in appearance and the impression you make can add 20 percent to your salary.

Wild animals don't need image consultants, but naturally assume the coloration of their environment in order to prey on instead of being preyed upon. By assuming the professional colorations of your future business environment, you will fit in colorfully and culturally and not only survive but potentially receive a higher salary offer.

Appropriate and Stylish Business Dress

- Business suits in blue, brown, black pinstripe, and camel (women only) are always appropriate.
- Colored shirts, blouses, and ties project energy, authority, and sophistication.
- High-quality leather shoes and portfolios are a must-have.
- Minimal jewelry and tasteful makeup are appropriate.
- Hair, beards, and mustaches all benefit from a stylish cut and even a touch-up with hair color.
- Use business-appropriate and stylish self-expression in your dress.
- Seek help from the professionals: hairstylists, career-transition consultants, image consultants, and clothing sales professionals.

All first impressions rely heavily on visual and nonverbal cues, which include posture, body language, voice, smell, and touch. Giving such heavy emphasis to first impressions may seem shallow, but it's of critical importance in your career search. Making a few small personal changes can cause you to be employed more quickly and command a higher salary. Believe me, a makeover is worth it!

To Create a Winning First Impression

❏ Are you displaying erect posture and walking vigorously?

❏ Are you projecting vocal energy and clarity on the phone and in person?

❏ Are there details of personal hygiene that you need to address?

❏ Is your business appearance appropriate and stylish?

What do you need to change to create a no-holds-barred positive first impression?

"Interviewers aren't necessarily looking to hire clones of themselves and their colleagues, but they do usually want to hire people who have a similar air about them."

—*Michelle Tullier,* The Unofficial Guide to Finding a Job

How to Achieve Awesome Interview Results

First of all, give yourself a little hug or pat on the back. Congratulations. You have already passed one or two major hurdles when you make it to the telephone or in-person interview.

Your first hurdle was having an awesome resume that met the approval of an automated scanner and a human scanner. (According to a recent article in *Smart Money*, only 5 to 25 percent of incoming online resumes are reviewed by humans. And scanning machines are beginning to screen on personal characteristics of their best and worst employees.) Making it this far should make you feel more self-confident.

The second and third hurdles are to effectively pass telephone and in-person interviews.

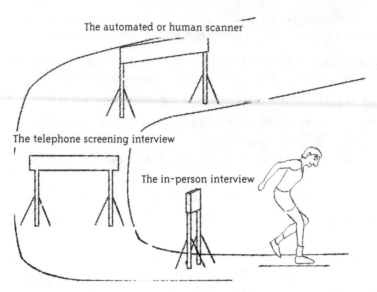

The automated or human scanner

The telephone screening interview

The in-person interview

Figure 9.2: Interview hurdles

Handling Telephone Interviews

One or multiple telephone interviews occur before the in-person interview takes place. This method saves time and money for all concerned and is used to screen out candidates that are not a good fit. The interview can be conducted by an external or internal recruiter or the hiring manager herself.

Here are some of the most important tips for participating in a successful telephone interview:

- Be prepared to answer the most difficult interview questions, having practiced them several times with a friend or coach. (These questions and suggested answers are covered on the next page.)

- Stand up for the interview if your energy tends to wane when seated.

- Smile when you're talking. Consider having a mirror to check your smile.

- Speak with animation and enthusiasm—you have only your voice to create a winning interview impression.

- Prepare questions to ask the interviewer.

Handling In-Person Interviews

Most people have a little anxiety before going to an interview. This is natural. The best way to handle this anxiety is to be well prepared: interview questions practiced ahead of time, interview outfit picked out and pressed, plenty of time allowed to locate the company, and so on.

Here are the main points to consider:

- **Know the company.** Do personal and Internet searches before the interview on the company and the hiring manager.

- **Review your accomplishments.** Be ready and comfortable during the interview to illustrate your strengths with specific examples. Be prepared to give additional examples beyond the points made in your resume. Remember to focus on the challenges you faced, the actions you took, and the results you obtained (using the CAR formula).

- **Create the right image by dressing conservatively and neatly.** Give careful attention to your personal grooming. Be on time or slightly early, so you will be relaxed, but not more than 10 minutes early.

- **Be enthusiastic, polite, and personable to everyone you encounter.** People hire people they like and the less-qualified person often gets a position over one who is more qualified but doesn't seem to care about people.

- **When you are meeting the person you came to interview, let him or her indicate where you should sit.** Bring a portfolio, resumes, references, and personal business cards. Ask for or exchange business cards to get the correct spelling, title, and phone and e-mail numbers.

- **Use open body language and avoid showing signs of nervousness.** Relax. Interviews are never fatal and can be enjoyable if you relax.

- **Get on the same wavelength with the interviewer.** Provide needed details and focus on ideas and concepts of interest to the interviewer.

- **Concentrate on your values.** Interviewers want to know if you can do the job, if you will do the job, and if the company can stand you while you do it.

- **Be positive and project optimism.** You will do your very best and your record speaks for your abilities.

- **Answer positively from the interviewer's point of view.** Modesty or timidity can be seen as weakness. Don't boast but don't be apologetic. Mistakes can be shown to have been valuable experiences. You can usually reframe a difficult question to give a response that does you credit.

- **Don't talk to an interviewer about personal problems.** Your problems will weaken your case.

- **Avoid premature salary discussions.** Don't talk money until your value has been built and understood. Don't seem concerned primarily with salary and benefits for yourself; these will be negotiated at an appropriate time. Research the range of salary for the position in advance.

- **Be an interested listener and observer.** What you say and ask should be relevant and of interest to the interviewer. Watch for signs of confusion, agreement, or strong interest, and react accordingly.

- **Concentrate on making a contribution in a team environment.** Competence alone does not sell; you must be seen as a person who will be productive in a compatible way.

- **Build interest toward your objective.** If conversation falters, ask questions to go further into areas in which the interviewer has shown interest. Try to have interest peak near the conclusion, then press for your objective: the next interview.

- **Write out questions in advance to ask the interviewer.** Examples include "When do you expect to have this position filled? What are the primary responsibilities for this position? Who would I report to? What kind of support will I have?" And so on.

- **Always protect the confidence of a past employer.** Be understanding of any difficulties the employer may have had, including those which caused you to leave. You may be talking to your future employer, and you are demonstrating how much consideration you will show him should problems arise.

- **Be yourself.** Don't be what you think someone else expects. Maintain your dignity and self-respect.

- **Let the interviewer control the interview.** Answer and ask questions with enthusiasm without over-talking or being too brief with your answers.

- **Close strongly.** Be prepared to close the interview with an approach such as "Based on what you know about me now, do you feel that I would be a good fit within this organization?"

Handling Tough Interview Questions

Earlier I mentioned that you should be prepared to answer the tough interview questions you might face. Following are examples of ways that you should answer these questions. Always answer positively from the interviewer's point of view. This is not a time for self-revelation about faults or missteps.

1. **Tell me about yourself.** Answer this by giving a brief description of your past career history in chronological order. "I have 10 years of experience in medical sales management with four of the top medical equipment companies. I am excellent in personal sales as well as mentoring and training others. I'm a native of Baltimore and have many healthcare contacts in this territory."

2. **Why did you leave or are leaving your last employer?** Give this a positive spin, such as, "My company has recently gone through a major organization and my position was affected. I am looking forward to..."

3. **Why do you want to work for us?** "I know from my contacts within the company that your employees are happy, that you have been in the black for nine consecutive years, that you are concerned about the environment, and that my skill set is an excellent match for this position."

4. **What do you have to offer over other candidates?** "I am always on time for work, meetings, deadlines, and projects. And I produce high-quality work."

5. **What are your salary expectations or your last salary?** Do your homework on the Internet to discover the fair market value of your potential position. You can evade the question one time by saying something such as "I am prepared to accept the fair market value for this position. Can you tell me your salary range?" When pressed a second time without the benefit of their salary range, give them the benefit of your research on the

range and ask them if this is what they had in mind. "I have researched the fair market value of this position in Atlanta and found it to be between $65,000 and $75,000. Is this what you have in mind?" If you are being interviewed by an external recruiter who insists on having your former salary, go ahead and share your last salary with a comment such as, "For the last three years, my salary averaged $72,000 plus a year-end bonus, which averaged $5,000."

6. **Tell me about a time you had a conflict or disagreement with a coworker and the outcome.** During the last two years that I was in charge of the Newark office, my supervisor asked me to cut my expense budget by 35 percent. He is an analytical kind of guy, so I sent him a letter outlining my position for not cutting expenses and instead increasing income. He accepted my proposal. Our relationship actually improved after this disagreement.

7. **Don't you think that you are overqualified for this job?** There are many positive ways to answer this question. One way would be, "I am challenged by this opportunity and am proud to bring my strengths of [insert your relevant strengths] to this position."

8. **Describe the characteristics of your best and worst boss.** Come down for a soft landing here. "I had one boss who was a true micromanager. She even told me what kind of luggage to travel with. I learned a lot from her, bought great carry-on luggage, and sometimes got my way. My favorite boss traveled with me to one sales presentation. When he saw that I knew how to handle it, he left me on my own unless I specifically asked him for advice or to attend a presentation. We were a successful team."

9. **Why have you changed jobs so frequently or why did you stay at your last company so long?** Use honesty with a positive spin, such as, "I have primarily been a contract accountant and these positions last from six months to two years."

10. **Where do you expect to be in five years?** "I expect to have performed well as a claims adjuster and to be promoted to a claims supervisor or above."

11. **What is your age or when did you graduate from college?** This is an age-discrimination question. One technique is to use

humor and not offend the interviewer. "I believe that I meet the minimum age requirements for this position."

12. **Why do you have that gap in your career history?** "After the technology bust in 2002–2001, it took me over a year to find another full-time opportunity. I went back to school to start on my MBA while continuing to look."

13. **Tell me about your greatest weakness or any comments of improvement that you have received on recent performance reviews.** "My greatest weakness is my own desire to come in early on projects. By setting such aggressive work deadlines, I please my clients, but I sometimes neglect having fun and relaxation with my family."

14. **How would you describe your leadership style?** "I am a collaborative leader and involve others concerned in important decisions."

15. **What is your educational background?** "I have a B.S. in Finance from the University of Michigan and received my PMI in 2009."

16. **What courses have you taken since college to update your skills?** "I have recently received a Supervisory Management Certificate from Kennesaw University."

17. **Tell me about your computer skills.** "I am excellent with all components of Microsoft Office, with special expertise in Word, Internet Explorer, and PowerPoint."

18. **How do you feel about reporting to a younger boss?** "I will enjoy working with a younger boss. My last boss was 15 years younger and we had an excellent rapport."

19. **Is this a career switch for you?** "Actually, I've always been a teacher in terms of adult learning and training and I've managed teenagers, so I see high school teaching as right up my alley."

20. **What is your dream job?** "My dream job is this administrative assistant job supporting key executives in a company I admire."

21. **What does success mean to you?** Best to be truthful and simple. "Success means to me to be happy and fulfilled in meaningful work." Or, "Success to me means making a lot of money for my employer." The latter works for a sales position. What

comes across as pseudo is something like, "Success means to me having every employee in the company, all clients, and my family happy all at the same time."

22. **Tell me about a project that you were unable to complete on time.** Technically speaking, this question is meant to draw out a time that you failed to meet a work deadline. If you do not want to raise a red flag, you can simply say that you have always met your work deadlines, but there was a time that you volunteered to make a Christmas candy house for your child's school and had to back out because of a tight work schedule.

23. **What else should I know about you?** "You should know that I will be a great fit within your organization because of my high energy level, my knowledge of current market conditions, and my results orientation." End with, "Based on what you know about me, now do you think I'll be a good fit within the organization?"

Putting It All Together

Like it or not, you are judged in the first 60 seconds of any meeting, so give it your best shot. Plan to stand out in the crowd. Create a visual, vocal, and total sensory presence that will make everyone in the room look at you admiringly when you enter. Watch for consistency in all aspects of your written, visual, and vocal presentation. Recruiters strongly declare that personal appearance and self-confidence are key factors in closing our own personal sale, landing a job.

The balance of power has shifted when you are invited to interview. Before the interview, the interviewer, recruiter, or employer holds about 75 percent of the power. When you are invited to interview, the power shifts more in your favor. This fact alone should increase your self-confidence.

CHAPTER 10

Negotiating Your Best Offer

Babcock and Laschever, the authors of *Women Don't Ask,* have found that "by not negotiating a first salary, an individual stands to lose more than $500,000 by age 60—and men are more than four times as likely as women to negotiate a first salary." (First salary here refers to every type of first salary: first salary with a new employer, first contract with a new client, first new hourly wage, and so on.)

In this chapter I answer three of the most important questions regarding salary and benefits negotiations:

- Why are people reluctant to negotiate salary and benefits?
- How effective are attempts to negotiate salary and benefits?
- What are the specific steps to use to successfully negotiate salary and benefits?

Then I show you three actual career-transition negotiations. You will also have an opportunity to participate in a virtual negotiation to prepare you for your own.

Why Are People Reluctant to Negotiate Salary and Benefits?

People are reluctant to negotiate salary and benefits because of lack of confidence in their ability to negotiate, perception that the negotiation process will be unpleasant or unsuccessful, and fear that they will lose the offer if they persist in negotiation. And recent surveys indicate that men are four times as likely as women to negotiate because they view negotiating as a sport, such as a tennis match, whereas women view it as an unpleasant experience, such as going to the doctor.

The good news is that by the time you finish this chapter you will understand that negotiation is an acquired skill that you can use effectively without fear. There will come a time when you will actually enjoy a negotiation. And you will appreciate that a successful negotiation is a win-win experience that can actually enhance the relationship between employer and employee—a relationship in which each party gains more respect for the other after negotiating.

When you receive a salary offer, your self-confidence soars, and from a negotiation standpoint the scales have tipped in your favor (see figure 10.1). How far the scales have tipped depends on multiple factors, including the employer's urgency in filling the position, whether you are currently employed, and the value the employer perceives in hiring you.

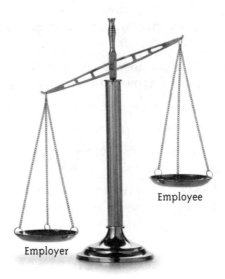

Employee

Employer

Before the Interview

During the Interview

At the Time of the Offer

Figure 10.1: The balance of power in salary negotiations.

How Effective Are Attempts to Negotiate Salary?

I strongly encourage all of my career clients to negotiate offers for full-time employment, contract employment, and all self-employment situations. I am pleased to say that 99 percent of my clients are successful in their negotiation efforts because they understand the right steps in negotiation and know what to say and do. They happily report that they have increased their salary, benefits, and self-confidence from negotiating job and contract offers.

I work with an average of six new career clients a month with career transition programs lasting from a couple of weeks to three months and more. The track record for clients who negotiate with my assistance is 99 percent success in obtaining one or more of their points of negotiation, including salary, bonus, vacation, moving expenses, car allowance, temporary housing expenses, and so on. I have coached only one client on negotiation techniques who decided not to negotiate his offer. He felt that his offer was fair market value; he was grateful to receive it, and he opted not to "rock the boat."

This chapter includes three actual successful negotiation scenarios that will help you appreciate how effective negotiation can be when you are prepared.

The Five Steps to a Successful Negotiation

To overcome the intimidation that comes with negotiation, it helps to have a process to follow. Following are my five steps to a successful negotiation of salary, benefits, and other contract elements.

1. Discover What You Are Worth

When you enter the job market or are seeking a contract or self-employment opportunity, research the value of your position in the city where the opportunity is located. Here are some examples of my clients who did just that:

- Sharon, a senior-level director of finance in Chicago, wanted to relocate to Boston. She used Salary.com (www.salary.com) to research the salary range for her position in Boston. We were both excited to determine that the midrange for her position was $246,090. Sharon further refined her fair market value by ordering a customized salary report, which accounted for her education, experience, and the size and type of organization she was targeting.

- My client Don had 10 years of successful experience in software sales in Atlanta. When he researched his salary on Indeed (www.indeed.com), he found a base salary of $113,000 and information that salaries were 8 percent higher in Atlanta than nationwide for this position. Don's was a very basic report.

- For LaTonya, an administrative assistant in Huntsville, Alabama, we found a salary range of $23,000 to $43,000 on SalaryExpert.com (www.salaryexpert.com).

When researching your salary online, look at a minimum of three different sources and decide whether the free or customized report is more appropriate for you. In higher-level positions, I would opt for the most complete report and pay for it. Make sure you take into account whether you are in an entry-level, midrange, or senior-level position.

2. Delay Revealing Your Salary Expectations

Internal and external recruiters will frequently ask you what you are making or what your salary expectations are, as early as their initial telephone screening interview. This is to literally screen you out if your salary expectations are not in the range the company has established. They may go so far as to say, "Would you be able to accept less?" Or "What is your bottom line?" They are already attempting to negotiate before offering you a position.

The way to handle the salary question when it first comes up is to say, "I am flexible with my salary and I'm expecting to earn fair market value for the position." Then ask them, "What is the salary range for this position?" If pressed to answer the salary question, respond with your research: "I have researched this position through two major salary research sites, and for my midlevel position the range is $78,000 to $85,000. Is this what you have in mind?"

Try to focus the discussion on the value you offer and postpone salary discussions until later in the interview process when you have established your value.

3. Handle External Recruiters and Applications

Many external recruiters and executive recruiters are paid by the employer based on a percentage of the applicant's first-year salary, so the recruiter has a vested interest in knowing that the salary you desire is in the range the employer will pay. When a recruiter asks about your salary requirements, provide your researched salary range first. The same rule applies to retained-search recruiters who are compensated on a negotiated fee from the employer that is also based on a percentage of the annual salary.

In the case of filling out an application that asks for salary, history or requirements, if you do not want to reveal your salary, you can often fill in the blank with "discuss in person." If this tactic does not work, answer the question truthfully based on the value of your last salary and bonus or your future salary expectations, depending on the question asked.

4. Wait 24 to 48 Hours Before Accepting or Negotiating the Offer

Always get your offer/offers in writing and ask for up to 48 hours to discuss the "wonderful" offer with your family. Always thank the employer for the offer. Then ask enough questions to understand the benefits, including medical insurance, vacation time, tuition reimbursement, 401(k), and so on.

Try to make an in-person appointment to respond to the written offer. Before your appointment, compare the features of the offer you have received to the features of the offer you desire by creating your own customized version of the chart in table 10.1. The difference between the offer and what you desire will be your points of negotiation.

Use a scale of 1 to 5, with 5 being the most important features and 1 being the least important. Compare your offer score to your desired score and highlight the areas for negotiation. Some areas, such as the commute and the 401(k), are not negotiable but are compensated for by other areas.

Table 10.1: Offer Evaluation Grid

Features	Desired Offer	Offer
Salary	$90,000 (5)	$80,000 (3)
Bonus	15% of sales (5)	12% of sales (4)
Challenging work	Yes (5)	Yes (5)
Vacation	4 weeks (3)	2 weeks (2)
401(k) match	25% (3)	10% (2)
Flex-time	Yes (4)	Yes (4)
Work from home office	Yes (2)	Yes (2)
Tuition reimbursement	Yes (1)	Yes (1)
Medical insurance	Small deductible (5)	Yes (5)
Commute	10 miles (4)	15 miles (3)
Total	**37**	**31**

5. Negotiate the Offer

Now we get to the "fun" part, the part of the offer negotiation that is both financially and emotionally rewarding. Imagine that you have made an appointment with the hiring manager for tomorrow afternoon. You have just completed your comparison chart. You know that you want to negotiate a raise in your salary, an increase in the percent of your bonus, and an increase in the length of your vacation. Otherwise, you like the offer and are prepared to accept it if you can gain satisfactory movement in the three key areas. This is your only offer on the table, by the way. Let's see how the meeting plays out.

You go in and shake hands with Ruben Irving, the hiring manager, and sit in the chair in front of his desk. You engage in small talk for a moment and then he asks you what you think about the offer. First, you thank him for the offer and tell him that you sincerely appreciate it and that you are excited about the possibility of working for the ABC Group. You go over all of the features of the position that are particularly pleasing to you, such as the challenge of the work, the medical insurance, the flexible hours, and the ability to work from your home on a part-time basis. These are the areas of agreement.

Then you indicate that you are prepared to join the organization if concessions can be made in other areas.

Ruben raises his eyebrows and asks you what other areas. You begin with your number-one priority, salary. You indicate that your expectations were for a base salary in the neighborhood of $90,000 based on your research of the fair market value for this position. He indicates that he is authorized to offer up to $85,000. You indicate that you will accept $87,000. He leaves the room to make a call and comes back with a revised offer of $87,000.

Next, you bring up the bonus and vacation. The hiring manager indicates that the bonus percent is set in concrete, but that he can go for three weeks of vacation. You are happy with the revised offer. You shake hands and ask for the new offer in writing. You accept it, walking away with an annual starting salary $5,000 higher than offered and an extra week of paid vacation worth $1,338. This negotiation was well worth the effort.

Sometimes the negotiations will take more than one meeting. Be patient and pleasant throughout. Know when to persist and when to turn down the offer if it is below your minimum requirements. Before negotiating the offer, establish your minimum requirements for accepting the offer. This will depend on other offers pending, your financial status, how long you have been in the job search, the state of the economy, and so on.

Real-Time Negotiation Scenarios

Now let's take a firsthand look at several exciting negotiation scenarios involving a variety of clients.

Weyman

When I first met Weyman, he was a mid-level executive with a major utility company. He felt under-challenged, underappreciated, and underpaid and wanted to substantially increase his salary, change his company, obtain a vice president or director position, and relocate from Atlanta to Colorado, Montana, Arizona, or New Mexico. His wish list was fueled by the fact that his kids were now out of school and it was time for him to maximize his career potential without sacrificing their school stability. Also, he and his spouse had always wanted to live in the West.

To Weyman's advantage, he had a track record of excellent career performance, two bachelor of science degrees, and a recent MBA. He presented himself well, dressed impeccably, and had a wide range of networking contacts, including current vendors. Despite all he had going for him, the challenge we faced was huge because of his expansive wish list and because we were entering a downturn in the financial sector.

Weyman and I began working together in October with his taking the BirkmanDirect. The assessment confirmed that he would be a good fit for a vice president of sales position, and I felt that he had enough significant transferable experience for me to create an executive resume that would be a close match to the position he desired. The Birkman assessment also assured both of us that Weyman would be self-directed, systematic, and energetic in his career search. The assessment revealed that he "can endure sustained opposition and is action oriented."

After we completed the resume, Weyman began targeted networking to companies of interest in the financial industry. We took a break over the holidays and then began again in earnest. In January, Weyman was well along in interviews with major companies either headquartered or having major offices in the West. There were many interviews out of town, including an international meeting in New York over an elegant dinner. (No, I was not invited.)

Later in January, frustration set in for both of us when company hiring timetables were slower than ours. It was hurry up and wait. Then at the end of January good news began to break, with offers in February from a well-known financial institution and a promising entrepreneurial energy company. We first evaluated both offers using a customized version of the negotiation chart in table 10.1.

After securing his offers in writing, Weyman went back to the major financial company and, after securing their salary offer of $125,000 base and an Assistant VP status, negotiated three months of out-of-state residence expenses, moving expenses, four weeks of vacation, a company vehicle, and a sign-on bonus of $11,000. The difference that his negotiation made was $4,100 extra in bonus, four weeks of vacation instead of two weeks of vacation ($5,208), three months instead of two months of out-of-state residence expense ($1,000), and a company vehicle ($30,000). He earned at least $40,000 more by carefully charting out how his offer differed from his desired offer and going back to the company to negotiate. It's amazing how the features add up.

I assisted in Weyman's offer evaluation and we verbally role-played the actual negotiation so that he would become confident in the execution. When I role-play an interview or negotiation with a client, I play the employer and the client plays the client, but then we switch and I play the employee so that they can hear how I would handle some of the more difficult parts of the negotiation.

What often get in the way of a successful negotiation are the fear factor and preconceived ideas that certain positions are nonnegotiable. What overcomes these obstacles is creating a chart in advance and practicing the negotiation in a role-play.

Not all negotiations have so much at stake; in fact, according to negotiation experts, the average salary negotiation gain is $4,000. I would be willing to spend a day in making a chart and practicing and executing a negotiation for $4,000 plus. Would you? And most of the gains I see exceed $4,000.

Luis

I mentioned earlier that 99 percent of my clients negotiate a number of factors: salary, bonus, location, vacation, and so on, but there is always the unusual situation when accepting a position without negotiation may be the way to go.

Luis was a senior software developer who was so unhappy and stressed at his last position that he quit, giving up all claims to severance or unemployment. He was married with two children and had a nonworking spouse with a difficult-to-insure medical condition. When he hired me, Luis had been out of work for six months and he and his family were under considerable financial stress.

I worked with Luis for two months, encouraging him, preparing his resume, doing interview practice, and identifying leads in his choice of relocation cities. The job market was slow at this point and it was not until five months after we began that Luis received a very fair offer in writing, which was in the midrange of the pay scale for a senior software developer. Luis called me to discuss his offer.

Luis's offer included 10 percent of his annual salary in relocation expenses, including temporary living expenses and moving expenses; substantial insurance benefits, medical and dental; two weeks of vacation that he had confirmed were nonnegotiable; a 401(k) match;

and a large tuition reimbursement. I congratulated him and we discussed negotiating the salary, the relocation expenses, and a sign-on bonus.

He told me that he felt that this position was "scarce"; he had been in the market for 11 months and that, with the length of time in the job search and his background of leaving the former company, he was grateful to get the offer. He thought the salary was fair in the midrange and that this type of position did not generally pay a bonus. Although this salary may have had some upward movement (the maximum range was about $13,000 higher), this company was going out on a limb to pay him about $8,000 in relocation expenses. Under the circumstances, I validated Luis's decision not to negotiate.

Always remember that negotiations should produce a win-win situation, where both parties feel that they have reached a satisfactory outcome.

Judy

Negotiation skills are useful in every aspect of our lives, not just in negotiating salary and benefits. We negotiate prices at flea markets, in malls, buying cars, with our children over treats and privileges, and with our family and friends over where to eat and what movie to see. Let's take a look at a final negotiation with a skeptical client who thought that her offer would not be negotiable. On this one, I'll let you participate in the negotiation.

Judy was the vice president of operations for a major cardiology practice. Her educational background included an RN designation and a recent B.S. in nursing, and she was currently enrolled in an MBA program. She had demonstrated success as a nurse and as a small-business owner/consultant and had comprehensive experience in large healthcare practices. She was single and had just completed her dream home after caring for an aging mother for five years. She appeared to be self-confident and well spoken and had many connections in the industry.

Her wish list was to associate herself with a large medical center involving a hospital and doctors' practices as a director or assistant director, where she had more room for growth in responsibility and salary. She didn't want to immediately relocate and wanted to continue in the financial lifestyle that she had built for herself.

At the end of two months of working together weekly through the career assessment, resume, and interview practice, Judy tried to convince me that in executive positions in medical practices, negotiation is not possible because salaries and benefits are set in concrete. Fortunately, my background was not in healthcare, so when she presented me with the offer she had received in writing, I took a fresh, creative approach.

The following chart contains Judy's wish list. I have filled in the offer she received. I would like for you to make your suggestions on her negotiation after reviewing her offer. Before you begin I will add that the beginning salary is not negotiable and Judy does not want to relocate at this point. Her commute is 180 miles round trip. How can she increase her financial gain? She sees no way, but really wants this job. It is at a major hospital with great advancement opportunities and wonderful people to work with.

Table 10.2: Judy's Offer

Features	Desired Offer	Offer
Salary	$120,000 (5)	$110,000 (4)
Bonus	Based on profits (5)	Based on profits (5)
Challenging work	Yes (5)	Yes (5)
Vacation	4 weeks (3)	4 weeks (3)
401(k) match	25% (3)	25% (3)
Advancement	Yes (5)	Yes (5)
Coworkers	Yes (7)	Yes (5)
Tuition reimbursement	Yes (3)	Yes (3)
Medical insurance	Small deductible (5)	Yes (5)
Commute	20 miles (4)	180 miles (1)
Relocate	No (2)	No (2)
Score	47	41

Be creative and list below Judy's main points for negotiation and how she should present them.

1. _____

2. _____

3. _____

I advised Judy that because she could not increase her base salary, she should ask for a 90-day review with the potential of increasing the salary based on a promotion and change in title for excellent performance. At her 90-day review, Judy's title was changed from Operations Vice President to Director of Operations and her salary was increased to $130,000. It was her choice to continue the commute for six months before deciding to move, so she negotiated a six-month mileage allowance. We figured that with this negotiation and her high performance, we netted her about $28,000 more than if she had continued to assume that her healthcare position was nonnegotiable.

Summing Up

What you have learned in this chapter is that you can increase your salary and benefits in the majority of offers by using planned and practiced negotiations. Negotiations are also important for the entrepreneur. Almost every week, I am negotiating with my clients to purchase additional services or executive coaching, and they are negotiating with me about exchanging one service for another. Negotiation is about getting what you've always wanted while allowing the person you negotiate with to feel that they have also gotten what they wanted. So to get what you want, you need to learn to negotiate win-win situations.

You have read the negotiation scenarios in this chapter, learned the important steps, and participated with me in Judy's negotiation. What are the most important points you have learned about negotiation? What are your key negotiation takeaways?

1. _____

2. _____

3. _____

Stephen Covey, in his *7 Habits of Highly Effective People,* stressed the habit "Begin with the End in Mind." This means that unless you know what the features of your ideal position will look like—such as the salary, vacation, location, personnel, and so on—you will not get what you want in your salary and benefits and you will not know what to negotiate for. So designing your chart of the salary and benefits you want before negotiations begin is an awesome way to begin to get the career you've always wanted.

I was an attorney and a vice president of sales and marketing before I was a career counselor. Here is the story of the first time that I negotiated my salary and bonus as vice president of sales and marketing. First, I called to make an appointment with our chief operating officer and flew from Atlanta to Detroit to meet with him.

Although I had not prepared a formal negotiation chart, I knew that I wanted to increase my base salary and my bonus percentage. He welcomed me and I sat in a chair in front of his desk. I experienced a mixture of confidence and fear. I knew that he wanted to keep me in my position because of my outstanding personal sales and the success of our Western region team, but I also knew that he could be stubborn and intimidating and say "no."

After a few minutes of small talk, he said to me, "I have been dreading this meeting because I know that you are a great negotiator." This comment shocked me and taught me that not all executives are skilled negotiators. (He probably assumed that my JD degree automatically made me a skilled negotiator.) And then he ended up giving me everything that I asked for in the negotiation: a substantial increase in base salary and bonus. The truth of the matter was that I was not a skilled negotiator at the time, but I figured "nothing ventured, nothing gained."

What you can learn from my own experience and that of my clients is that with a little bit of practice, you may become a more skilled negotiator than the hiring manager, regardless of his or her title.

Negotiation is exciting and financially rewarding. If you enjoy computer or board games or any kind of strategic competition, you will begin to see this as Career Monopoly. The skills you gain in negotiation will serve you well in your career transition, during performance reviews, and in all promotional opportunities.

CHAPTER 11

Too Young to Quit Working: Careers for Post-Retirement Years

Twenty years ago, my brother-in-law Bob told me that he never expected to retire. I thought, "That is ridiculous. Why would someone want to continue working in their 60s and 70s unless they were in financial need?" My own plans were to retire at 55 from a highly compensated corporate sales management job, to enjoy family and friends, and to travel to exotic international destinations. Little did I know that when I reached 55, I would be saying, "Forget about retirement. I'll work as long as I want. I can work and still enjoy family, friends, and travel to exotic international destinations." And I certainly didn't know when I decided to continue working that the 2008–2009 financial tsunamis would provide me with additional reasons to keep working. Like many of you, I watched my retirement savings disappear and my home value decline.

"Retirement has been redefined. It is no longer an automatic shift in gears from work to non-work at a set age. It is, rather, a voluntary withdrawal from the work force at the age that best suits an individual's abilities, interests, and career plans."

—The End of Mandatory Retirement, *Walker and Lazer*

When Is the Right Age to Quit Working?

The question is not really "When is the right age to quit working," but "what work do you want to do at your current age?" Mandatory retirement was widespread in the 1960s and 1970s, but in 1978 the U.S. Congress outlawed mandatory retirement before age 70, and in 1986 abolished it altogether. Authorities indicate that this extension of the Age Discrimination in Employment Act (ADEA) was brought about to raise labor force participation and to create a more flexible definition of retirement. Unfortunately, many older workers and potential employers have not bought into this flexible definition of retirement. Some employers still engage in subtle and not-so-subtle age discrimination, and a few older workers engage in *self-*discrimination by entertaining negative thoughts about their age, their career choice, what others will say, and so on.

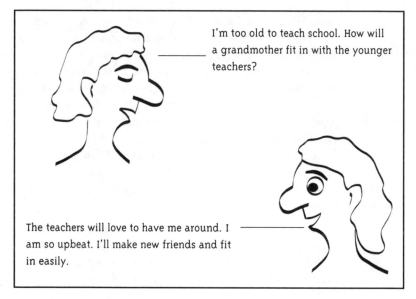

Figure 11.1: Negative Stereotype: I will be a cultural misfit because of my age.

A recent AARP survey of people 45 and older indicates that 57 percent of people working or looking for a job who had lost money in the market during the past year indicated they were delaying retirement. The ages of 55, 60, 65, 70, or even 75 are only arbitrary numbers that have increasingly less significance in today's world. Couples start families in their 30s and 40s, and we are experiencing an exponential increase in the number of centenarians (people over 100).

Life seems to be starting later and continuing longer. The number of centenarians in the United States is doubling every decade. According to the latest Wikipedia report, the United States had 79,000 centenarians and projections are that the number will rise to 834,000 by 2050. You may be one of them. For projections on how long you will live, check out www.livingto100.com. I took the quiz and found out that I may live to be 113.7 years, so I am even more motivated to keep working. I also discovered that I needed to work on my stress management and drink green tea for a number of health benefits. Now I drink green tea concentrate in my morning juice and reduce my stress with walking, yoga, and massage. And yes, there is the occasional nap.

Your actual age number has little significance in your "ageless" employment status, but what does have significance is that you choose work that supports your emerging preferences and values. For some people, making a certain annual income will be a continuing necessity; for others, time flexibility or being involved in meaningful paid or unpaid work is critical.

You will be more content in your career choices if you incorporate your preferences and values. Take a moment to complete the following worksheet for some real eye openers.

Rating Your Preferences and Values

First, rank these preferences and values on a scale of 1 to 10, with 1 being the most important to you. Feel free to have more than one of the same values. Next, circle your top three.

Career Preference/Value	Fulfillment Score
High income potential	_____
Time flexibility	_____
Opportunity for recognition/ encouragement/approval	_____
Opportunity to contribute/ give back/provide meaning	_____
Opportunity for self-expression/ input/creativity	_____
Benefits: medical/retirement	_____
Career autonomy/empowerment/ choice	_____
Expression of existing strengths/ interests/abilities	_____
Development of new competencies	_____
Challenge/stimulation/learning	_____
Activity/action/fun/variety	_____
Stability/affiliation/teamwork	_____
Power/leadership/responsibilities	_____
Not physically challenging	_____
Other: _____	

When you are evaluating job or career opportunities or considering self-employment, use your top three preferences/values to determine whether the potential opportunity fulfills what you consider most important. You will eliminate later disappointments by honoring your personal preferences and values.

Evaluating Some of the Best Retirement Career Options

By now, you've learned that the term "retirement careers" is an oxymoron in itself but does have some merit in describing those careers you choose after you are 55, 60, 65, or even 70. The best retirement career options are those that match your preferences and values. Many different mature career options are available, and the following list groups them in four categories:

- Corporate or organizational employment: full-time, part-time, and contract

- Temporary and seasonal employment

- Self-employment, including franchises, business ownership, and consulting opportunities

- Volunteer opportunities

- Survival employment (temporary employment that you take to pay the bills, but don't enjoy)

Each category has its merits, depending on your own preferences and values. In fact, you may want to combine several of these categories into a new category: concurrent employment. This fast-growing employment trend can be a combination of jobs from two or more of the preceding categories. For example, Dick, a self-employed CPA, works part-time from his home office as a consultant and volunteers as a SCORE counselor for the Small Business Administration.

Corporate or Organizational Employment

Believe it or not, many people love their corporate or organizational full-time employment and never want to leave. Such a person is my cousin Jane, who has been playing bass in the Atlanta Symphony since she was a teenager. At 80, she is still playing and is going for a spot in the Guinness Book of World Records as the symphony member of a major orchestra with the longest career. If you love your work and can keep up, why not stay with it?

For most of us who want time flexibility, medical benefits, or action and fun, a part-time or contract position may be made-to-order. Seniors who seek fresh challenges will find employers glad to help them out.

Many companies enjoy hiring former employees for part-time or contract work. Stan had been a successful outside insurance sales professional for a major insurance brokerage. He contacted the company about the possibility of doing promotional work for them. Instead of doing promotional work, he landed a research contract to identify and obtain full sales lead information involving major Southeast businesses with $1,000,000 and over in sales in selected industries. This contract work was quite a challenge with a tight deadline, involving the need to separate all leads by their offices and to record the information in Excel spreadsheets. Stan hired two people to help him with clerical and research tasks. The project came in on time, and he made a bonus for his efforts.

I asked Stan to rate his contract and part-time insurance assignment in terms of his preferences and values. The table on the next page lists Stan's values and rates the project in terms of those values. 1 represents his top preferences and values. 10 represents the least.

Stan confided in me that he had enjoyed many contract assignments with his old firm, but this was not one of them. He had autonomy and power and was well paid, but the deadline and the need to push his subcontractors made it a nightmare experience. Stan's top three values are

1. Self-expression and creativity

2. Expression of strengths, interests, and abilities

3. Time flexibility

But, as you can see from his ratings of this contract assignment, Stan's top three values were not fulfilled in this assignment. He admits that his desire for fast money caused him to take an assignment he should have passed on.

In considering working in a corporate environment on a contract or part-time basis, make sure that the opportunity represents an expression of your three most important values.

Table 11.1: Corporate or Organizational Employment: Contract or Part-Time

Stan's Career Preference/Value	Corporate or Organizational Employment: Contract or Part-time	Fulfillment Score
High income potential	Depends on the job	1
Time flexibility	No	10
Opportunity for recognition/ encouragement/approval	Yes, and bonus	10
Opportunity to contribute/ give back/provide meaning	Depends on the job	5
Opportunity for self-expression/ input/creativity	Depends on the job	5
Benefits: medical/retirement	In some cases	0
Career autonomy/ empowerment/choice	Depends on the job	3
Expression of existing strengths/interests/abilities	Yes	8

(continued)

(continued)

Stan's Career Preference/Value	Corporate or Organizational Employment: Contract or Part-time	Fulfillment Score
Development of new competencies	Yes	8
Challenge/stimulation/learning	Yes	2
Activity/action/fun/variety	Yes	9
Stability/affiliation/teamwork	No	0
Power/leadership/responsibilities	Depends on the job	I
Not physically challenging	Depends on the job	4
Other:		

What if you are not sure what you want to do but want some career stimulation? Check out these Web sites for seniors:

- Seniors4Hire (www.seniors4hire.org)
- Workforce 50 (www.workforce50.com)
- SnagAJob (www.snagajob.com)
- AARP: Top 20 Retirement Jobs (www.aarp.org/money/work/articles/top_20_retirement_jobs.html)
- Retired Brains (www.retiredbrains.com)

I found jobs on these sites that I might have pursued if I did not have my own career-transition business or if I needed quick money. One of the most unusual was testing mattresses and writing up a report for $30 to $40 per report. One of the advantages of being in what some are calling "the third age" is that you don't have to work at any one career longer than you enjoy it. You can be a dilettante and change careers. Or you can work at multiple careers at the same time, what I call concurrent careers. The above AARP link lists 20 of the Top Employers that are interested in hiring mature workers along with the credentials required.

Temporary and Seasonal Employment

Two years ago, I volunteered to do a career workshop at a local church. As we were doing preparatory work for the employment experience section of our resumes, Laura said she had a problem: For the last seven years, she had two or three different employers a year. At first, I was astounded and thought that she had been jumping employers or had been terminated. At that time, I had been working with more traditional corporate clients and had not yet experienced the growing phenomenon of older workers who consistently work in temporary and seasonal employment.

Laura was 56 years old and was professionally trained as a dental assistant. After she divorced and moved to another city, she was tired of the dental assistant occupation and began selecting temporary and seasonal employment as she found it. This year Laura had worked for the IRS as a data-entry clerk during tax season and at the Crowne Plaza hotel as a special events bartender during the Christmas season and for parties. She is consistently independently employed as an elder caregiver, and works as a small-business office assistant when needed. Let's take a look at how these temporary and seasonal positions fulfill her preferences and values.

Table 11.2: Temporary and Seasonal Employment Career Options

Career Preference/Value	Temporary and Seasonal Employment	Fulfillment Score
High Income Potential	Moderate, but you can work many hours and receive overtime at $10–15 per hour	5
Time flexibility	No, unless you take time off	10
Opportunity for recognition/ encouragement/approval	Yes	6
Opportunity to contribute/ give back/provide meaning	Yes, depending on assignment	2
Opportunity for self-expression/ input/creativity	Not often	9
Benefits: Medical/retirement	No, except IRS provides medical benefits opportunity	0

Career autonomy/empowerment/choice	Not frequently	8
Expression of existing strengths/interests/abilities	Depends on the job	5
Development of new competencies	Yes, if you select new challenge	4
Challenge/stimulation/learning	Yes, depending on the job	4
Activity/action/fun/variety	Yes, with multiple jobs; but some are boring	3
Stability/affiliation/teamwork	Not consistently	9
Power/leadership/responsibility	Depends on the job	8
Not physically demanding	Depends on the job	8

As you look at the chart on Laura's seasonal and temporary work, ask yourself whether this option meets your career preferences and values. For Laura, the cons are the lack of benefits and the fact that working long hours is physically demanding.

You can make as much income in seasonal and temporary work as in some full-time work in a corporate environment if you are willing to work long hours. Or you can supplement your retirement income or Social Security income by working a more limited number of hours. As to whether this is a good retirement option for later years, I would say it depends on your physical endurance, mental agility, and personal aspirations. I do not see Laura working 80 hours a week after she is 65. I see her socking her money away, investing well, and considerably reducing her hours.

You can also find numerous temporary employment opportunities if you have good computer, writing, sales, and project-management skills. Check out www.tjobs.com and www.net-temps.com to connect with temporary employment agencies that you can find in the *Yellow Pages* and on the Internet. I have found incredibly interesting jobs on these two sites.

Self-Employment

Chapter 3 looked at entrepreneurial possibilities, including franchise ownership, consulting, speaking, training, buying a business, and starting your own business. These options are also a possibility for your post-retirement career plans.

Of a group of 15 to 20 adjunct career counselors at a well-known career transition firm, at least 75 percent are also self-employed as consultants and in other concurrent positions that support personal preferences and values. The median age is 55, and some consultants have continued to work into their 70s.

I have noticed an employment and a gradual unemployment pattern. When consultants are first employed, they frequently opt for a 40-plus-hour week. As they become older and more experienced, they seem to become less satisfied with a 9-to-6 workweek and go to a four-day week or less. This trend seems to be natural and positive. You don't have to quit. Just reduce your corporate work hours when you want to pursue your own business or hobbies.

Eleanor was a career-transition consultant and an excellent presenter in her 50s who taught a course titled "Entrepreneurship." Eleanor went from a five-day workweek to a four-day week, and then moved to North Carolina to pursue her dream of being part of and living in a spiritual/healing community. When she left, she remarked to me, "I have been encouraging others to pursue their dream. Now it's time for me to pursue my own."

It has been eight years since Eleanor left her corporate career to pursue self-employment. She intentionally retained her corporate connection part-time but shifted her emphasis to her life- and career-coaching business. Reducing her work hours before she moved gave her time to incubate and to tap into what she really wanted to do.

What Eleanor didn't realize when she moved to a somewhat rural community in North Carolina was that her life- and career-coaching business would be harder to build outside of a major city. Her community has many retirees, and few business and professional clubs and associations. Opportunities to promote her business are 45 to 55 minutes away. For the moment, she is relying on former clients, networking, word of mouth, and doing most of her coaching over the phone and by e-mail. She has developed a formal advertising campaign, including brochures, Web site, and newspaper advertisements.

Eleanor's advice to the budding entrepreneur is this: "Starting a business takes a lot longer than you might expect. Do as much as possible while you are working part-time to ease the financial drain and enable you to get on your feet sooner."

Let's take a look at how self-employment has fulfilled Eleanor's values and preferences: Her top three values and preferences are rated and shaded, and all other career preference values are rated, with 1 being her top preference/value and 10 being her least.

Table 11.3: Self-Employment Career Options

Career Preference/Value	Self-Employment	Fulfilment Score
High income potential	Yes, if pursued	4
Time flexibility	Yes	4
Opportunity for recognition/ encouragement/approval	Yes, if needed	0 (not required)
Opportunity to contribute/ give back/provide meaning	Yes	2
Opportunity for self-expression/ input/creativity	Yes	1
Benefits: medical/retirement	None, but can supplement by partial corporate employment	0 (not required)
Work autonomy/empowerment/choice	More than corporate, but consumer and client driven	0 (not required)
Expression of strengths/interests/abilities	Yes	3
Development of new competencies	Yes	4
Challenge/stimulation/learning	Yes	5
Activity/action/fun/variety	Yes	6
Stability/affiliation/teamwork	Moderate	0 (not required)
Power/leadership/responsibility	Yes	0 (not required)
Not physically demanding	Yes	5

As you review the chart on self-employment career options, ask yourself whether this option meets your top three preferences and values. Remember that you can be self-employed and fulfill different values and options than Eleanor.

Volunteer Opportunities

It is wonderful to think of the wide range of volunteer jobs/activities available for those who no longer need income. You have probably heard seniors say, "I'm busier now than when I was working full time." So what are they doing?

Jan is an example of a senior who is really enjoying herself. She is one of my friends who has been retired from her profession as an environmental engineer for nine years. She has astutely managed her investments with the help of her brother, a financial planner, and does not have ongoing financial needs to fund through employment. I remember asking her at our last lunch together, "What are you doing with your time?"

"Well, I'm painting a nursery in my home for my new grandchild. The ceiling is the worst! And I'm planning my next birthday party. It's another big one! I'm planning on having a band and lots of good food."

When I asked Jan about her volunteer activities, I found out that she volunteers in five different activities: She tutors an inner-city child several days a week, started a butterfly garden for the school, has become a Master Gardener, volunteers at her church, and volunteers for the native plant society. All in all, she spends at least a day a week in volunteer activities. Sounds like a busy life! Jan has a wide cadre of friends and also travels extensively. Jan is a cancer survivor who knows that life is precious, and each day has special meaning.

When I asked Jan and Wayne, another friend, for their experiential advice on volunteer opportunities, they said to choose those that relate to your areas of interest, preference, and values. Both are interested in nature and community service. I also asked both what career they would choose if their financials changed and they needed an income. Jan said that she would do landscape consulting. Although she cannot advertise her Master Gardener status, she has already provided this service as part of a church auction. Wayne indicated that he would be a paid naturalist and canoe guide on the Chattahoochee River.

Volunteering Opportunities Recommended by Jan and Wayne
■ Volunteer tutoring in reading and ESL (English as a second language) opportunities
■ Spontaneous volunteering for friends in need
■ Mission opportunities through a church
■ Providing meals at a local "homeless shelter"
■ Volunteering as a nature guide
■ Volunteering as a member of a native plant society
■ Working to increase voter registration

Let's see how Jan's preferences and values are expressed in her volunteer work.

As you rank your career preferences and values, remember that yours will be different from Jan's.

Volunteer activities are listed weekly in the newspapers. You can search for opportunities online by typing the keywords "volunteer activities," along with your city name, into your favorite search engine. Most churches offer national and international volunteer opportunities, and Cross-Cultural Solutions (www.crossculturalsolutions.org) offers international volunteer opportunities without a specific religious connection.

Table 11.4: Volunteer Opportunities

Career Preference/Value	Volunteer Opportunities	Fulfillment Score
High income potential	None	0
Time flexibility	Yes	6
Opportunity for recognition/encouragement/approval	Can be informal	8
Opportunity to contribute/give back/provide meaning	Yes	1
Opportunity for self-expression/input/creativity	Yes	9
Benefits: medical/retirement	No	0
Career autonomy/empowerment/choice	Yes	9
Expression of existing strengths/interests/abilities	Yes	2
Development of new competencies	Yes	4
Challenge/stimulation/learning	Yes	6
Activity/action/fun/variety	Yes	3
Stability/affiliation/teamwork	Yes	7
Power/leadership/responsibilities	No	0
Not physically challenging	Depends	5
Other:		

Enjoying a Career in Your "Third Stage of Life"

A career in the years after your 55th birthday can be the most satisfying time of your entire life. It's a time for self-assessment; a time to pause and evaluate how your preferences and values will play out in a corporate or organizational environment, in self-employment, and in volunteer work.

You have the opportunity to excel at any age and be increasingly accepted in many employment and organizational venues. Not only can you make money to support the lifestyle you desire, but you can also self-actualize again and again and again, reinventing yourself and fulfilling lifelong dreams. You can change careers or you can have multiple concurrent careers. It's up to you.

According to Ronald Kotulak in *Inside the Brain: Revolutionary Discoveries of How the Mind Works* (Kotulak, Andrews McMeel), people do not lose massive numbers of brain cells as they age. The brain's functions simply get rusty with disuse. He describes a number of well-documented research studies that indicate that keeping your mental fires ablaze is within your control.

Employment and volunteer activities can provide many of these brain stimulants:

- Reading
- Engaging in age-appropriate strenuous physical activity
- Traveling
- Participating in cultural events
- Engaging in continuous education
- Participating in clubs and professional associations
- Gaining satisfaction from accomplishments
- Showing willingness to change
- Feeling that what you do makes a difference in the lives of others

Jeff Justice, 57, owner of Corporate Comedy and a colleague in the corporate training aspect of my business, regenerates himself in his work. When we travel together, he is not in his room, mindlessly zonking out on TV, but is practicing tai chi to increase his balance and painting difficult Chinese brushstroke bamboo to stimulate his brain. On the same trip, you might find me painting folk-art animals, practicing yoga, and walking and running four miles.

In one of my seminars, I challenged participants to consider their future work/lifestyle by asking questions. One of the questions I asked was this:

> If you could choose the most exciting/glamorous career, what would you choose?

Today I was interviewed by CNN anchor Tony Harris on the topic of career networking. This interview fueled one of my lifelong dreams to be the Dr. Gail of career transition. After the shoot, Tony and I compared notes on our next lifelong dreams—easy for him to say, as his recent shootings have been in the Andes, whereas my next shooting will be at a local chamber of commerce. But as they say and I know, "It's not over until it's over."

I posed this question to one of my older clients who was trying to figure out what he wanted to do next. He said that he wanted be a paid naturalist. He is a volunteer naturalist now at the Chattahoochee Nature Center. His glamour version of a paid naturalist is to lead exotic adventure trips. After talking for an hour or so, we decided that he would start with outdoor adventure canoe trips. These plans justify his recent purchase of a third canoe and a cool new pair of water sandals.

You are never too old to adopt a version of your dream. One of my very wise friends, Susan, a psychologist, encourages us to look for the essence of what we want. Wayne wanted to lead exotic adventure trips. These trips didn't have to begin on the Amazon but could start at a river landing three miles from his home. Think about how you can achieve the essence of what you want. Do something immediately to support your dream.

What Is Your Impossible Dream?

Take a quiet moment and answer these questions for yourself for a preview of future possibilities:

1. If you were beginning your career all over again, what career would you choose?

_____

_____

_____

2. If you no longer had financial need, what would you do as a career or volunteer activity?

_____

_____

_____

3. If you had no physical or age limitations, what career would you choose?

_____

_____

_____

4. If you could choose the most exciting or glamorous career, what would you choose?

_____

_____

_____

5. What is the first way that you will manifest your dream?

_____

_____

_____

INDEX